S0-AXR-970

"An indispensable primer for retailers who don't want to get left in the dust of the Information Age."
—**Don Peppers,** co-author of *The One to One Future: Building Relationships One Customer at a Time*

"The day when *Customer Specific Marketing* is a condition of entry to retailing is not far off. Brian Woolf is a globally acknowledged expert on the technique and its implementation. In this book he enthusiastically shares the fruits of many years of intensive research and work in the field, backed up by real life examples. Wrapped up in a fresh, easy style, all the do's, don'ts and how to's are there. If you are really serious about retailing you will not put this book down until you have finished it."
—**Robin Clark,** Editor, *Customer Loyalty Today,* Somerton, England

"In the face of severe competition, we have succeeded in increasing our sales and bottom line results. There is no question that we owe this in great part to our involvement in *customer specific marketing*. Brian Woolf has been the guiding light behind our program and continues to carry the torch showing the way. He's our hero!"
—**Peter V. ("Greg") Gregerson, Jr.,** CEO, Gregerson's Foods Inc., Gadsden, Alabama

"Brian Woolf continues to lead our industry into a new era of relationship and loyalty marketing. His keen insight into this evolving, new method of marketing will revolutionize the way marketing dollars will be spent in our industry."
—**Jim Ukrop,** CEO, Ukrop's Super Markets, Richmond, Virginia

"Brian Woolf is to be commended for compiling an extremely useful 'how-to' handbook that is a must for any retailer, regardless of industry, who is looking to build stronger customer relations and bring dollars to their bottom line. I work with retailers from many industries including apparel, hard goods, soft goods, jewelers, restaurants, and resorts, and I highly recommend this book to each of these niches."
—**Claude A. Johnson,** President, Retail Resources Inc, Lyndhurst, New Jersey

"Incredible! Fascinating research and information on a topic that is truly valuable to any service industry. Definitely will be the new way of marketing."
—**Gary L. Mead,** Owner, Mi Amore Pizza & Pasta, Lompoc, California

"*Customer Specific Marketing* is a terrific book. Brian Woolf shows how retailers can profit by rewarding the right customer. Writing about electronic marketing with authority, he has produced an extremely well written book that is a pleasure to read, filled with interesting anecdotes and specific examples. Brian explains how to get started, pitfalls to avoid, and how to measure progress. This outstanding book will change the way retail stores will deal with their customers."
—**Arthur Hughes,** Executive VP of ACS, Inc, author of *The Complete Database Marketer and Strategic Database Marketing.*

"Nobody has devoted more energy than Brian Woolf in gathering information on card marketing. This book is a *must read* for <u>anyone</u> in retailing."
—**Dan Lescoe,** VP Sales & Marketing, Big Y Foods Inc, Springfield, Massachusetts

"I wish that we had met Brian Woolf 40 years ago. Our *customer specific marketing* has changed the way we view our business, suppliers, and customers. We are much closer to our customers, enabling us to understand their needs. It's as if we are in a whole new industry. All of our promotions, our entire way of marketing, is based on our customer club approach, Club DLM. Hats off to Brian Woolf!"
—**Norman Mayne,** CEO, Dorothy Lane Market, Dayton, Ohio

"After living and breathing this form of marketing within our own business for the last three years, and then to read this book—I suddenly realized how much I still had to learn about this new and exciting way to build a better business."
—**Roger Morgan,** Managing Director, Morgan's Tuckerbag Supermarkets, Melton, Victoria, Australia

"This book is the perfect tool to navigate retailers in their effort to establish the one-to-one relationship that will be the cornerstone of the markets of the future."
—**Kevin Doris,** COO, Gerland's Food Fair Inc., Houston, Texas

"There is nothing so powerful in marketing as a well executed *customer specific marketing* program. There is no one more knowledgeable on the subject than Brian Woolf. This terrific book takes electronic marketing to the next level."
—**Bill Brodbeck,** CEO, Dick's Supermarkets, Platteville, Wisconsin

"This book is an easy read for anyone who wants to understand frequent shopper programs. It's written in such a way that it will be valuable to an experienced reader, a novice, or anyone who just wants to know what it's all about."
—**Carlene A. Thissen,** President, Retail Systems Consulting, Naples, Florida

"The strategies and tactics which made us successful yesterday won't make us successful tomorrow. *Customer specific marketing* will unquestionably provide us solutions for tomorrow's success."
—**Tom Lowe,** Vice President Marketing, Price Chopper, Schenectady, New York

"Brian Woolf has a genius for making the complicated simple. If we had this book when we started our databased marketing program in 1991, we would have shortened our learning curve considerably, and saved countless dollars in the process."
—**Al Lees Jr.,** Chairman/CEO, Lees Supermarket, Westport, Massachusetts

"I warmly endorse this book by Brian Woolf which describes how *customer specific marketing* is beginning to allow retailers to manage their most valuable asset—their customers. This change will have a profound impact on the way retailers compete and will help to secure a solid position for store-based retailing as we move into the information age."
—**Willard R. Bishop,** President, Willard Bishop Consulting Ltd., Barrington, Illinois

"*Customer Specific Marketing* is a fantastic panoramic presentation of the most powerful conceptual change in free world marketing since the coming of modern communications technology.

"In one treatise, Brian Woolf has skillfully captured a universe of ideas, organized them into a compelling case for differentiated marketing, and backed up theory and concept with hard facts and concrete ideas about how to execute the concepts."
—**Roger E. Stangeland,** Director and Chairman Emeritus, the Vons Companies Inc., Pasadena, California

"This book is a road-map to the future of retailing—a future where we all compete for the loyalty of our customers, not just for their business this week. If you want to get beyond mere lip-service to this exciting concept, Brian Woolf shows you the way."
—**Feargal Quinn,** managing director of Superquinn, Ireland

"Finally, a way to translate the 'information revolution' into actionable data. Brian Woolf's book puts the retailer in charge of his destiny—indeed, it makes retailing fun again! *Customer specific marketing* has enabled us to solidify our business and our customer relationships in the face of some of the toughest competition in the US supermarket industry. I would not want to be in the supermarket business without it."
—**Gary Hawkins,** CEO, Green Hills Farms, Syracuse, New York

Customer Specific Marketing

THE NEW POWER IN RETAILING

BRIAN P. WOOLF

How to order additional copies of this book:

- call (800) 247-6553, anytime, or
- call Raphel Marketing, (609) 348-6646, or
- contact your local bookstore, or
- use the fax order form on page 249

For quantity discounts, please call USA (609)-348-6646

To order in Australia ...*call:* (03)-9743-4411
To order in the UK...*call:* 01458 274 444

Bookstores may order from the 800 number, above.

Dedication

I dedicate this book to those pioneers in *Customer Specific Marketing,* scattered around the world, from whom I have learned so much. My warmest thanks to each of them for sharing their experiences and insights and for the many enjoyable discussions as we set out along this fascinating new retail path.

CUSTOMER SPECIFIC MARKETING
Copyright © 1996 by Brian P. Woolf.

All rights reserved. Except for the usual review purposes, no part of this work may be reproduced or transmitted in any form or by any means, electronic or mechanical, including photocopy, recording, or any information retrieval system without the written permission from the publisher.

Printed in the United States of America by Cadmus Publishing, Richmond, Virginia.

Library of Congress Cataloging-in-Publication Data
96-060299

ISBN: 1-888-051-02-7
1. Marketing. 2. Management

Woolf, Brian P.
Customer Specific Marketing

Also by Brian P. Woolf
Shrinking the Corporate Waistline © 1992

Published by Teal Books, 6 Parkins Lake Court, Greenville, SC 29607-3628, USA. To order books call: (800) 247-6553

Contents

Preface

In 1993 I was privileged to be selected by the Coca-Cola Retailing Research Council to study the experiences of food retailers who had frequent shopping cards. With the invaluable assistance of a research associate, Wanda Shive, I spent six months, full-time, speaking to and/or visiting 83 companies that account for two-thirds of US supermarket sales. The resulting report was *Measured Marketing: A Tool to Shape Food Store Strategy**.

The biggest surprise was how little we really know about our customers. For example: how often do they *actually* visit our stores? (A lot less than we thought!) How many stop shopping with us each year? (A surprisingly large number!) We also discovered that our best customers not only visit us the most often, but also spend the most on each visit! The report's title reflected another major insight—that the intelligent use of customer information can play a decisive role in reshaping a retailer's strategy.Because the systematic gathering of customer information was new to most retailers—the technology genie enabling this is only recently out of its bottle—the report's findings raised many new questions. One, in particular, kept challenging me: given the typical food retailer's low profit margin of about 1% of sales, how can he afford to gather customer information and then profitably transform it into a competitive advantage?

This book is dedicated to answering that question.

*Available from the Coca-Cola Corporation by calling 1-800-438-2653.

Introduction

This book is about change. Profitable change. For some companies, highly profitable change. It's about how some food retailers have taken information about their customers, which has not been readily available until recently, and are using it to run their businesses with significantly greater confidence and success than in the past.

You will read how this information has shattered some of the key assumptions which have traditionally guided retailers in their decision making. (For example, we now know that over the course of a year, the top 20% of a food retailer's customers spends fifty times the amount of its bottom 20%.) You will learn why the use of this new knowledge is not only possible—but absolutely essential for success today.

Mass marketing, with its *one price fits all* approach, has been rendered obsolete by the sheer power of customer information—information which enables retailers to offer different price and benefit packages to their different customers and then measure its effectiveness in an easy, cost-effective way. Such differentiation is called *customer specific marketing*.

Is there pain involved in this change? Yes—but the pain is primarily in the minds of top management as they replace their mantle of assumptions, woven over many years, with a different way of viewing their business. For these executives, it's not so much accepting that *all customers are not equal*, than it is translating this fact into business practices that creates great anxiety.

Norman Mayne, chief executive officer of Dorothy Lane Market, Dayton, Ohio, is legendary in the food retailing industry for the emphasis placed on customers and service in his two stores. He is invited to speak all over the world about his company. For three years, he debated and worried about what the practice of customer specific marketing might do to the image of his family business, which has been handed down from one generation to the next. In 1995, he finally made the transition. His anxieties rapidly disappeared, and he now emphatically states that he would never go back to "the old ways." Recently, he wrote me ...

We have drastically cut back our cherry pickers. In fact, the total transaction count in our stores is down from last year—but our same-store sales and gross profits are up! We have eliminated print advertising completely. Our bottom line is up significantly over last year— thanks to our Club DLM, which has been in existence only six months!

What a transformation! What amazing results!—But not really! What Norman Mayne and his team at Dorothy Lane have achieved is being duplicated all around the world. I know executives, in companies ranging from the smallest to the largest in their respective countries, who can relate similar experiences.

This book is based on their experiences. It is based on facts, not theory. Its purpose is to share with you *what* these retailers are doing and *how* they are doing it so that you, too, may successfully embrace customer specific marketing as your core strategy.

Even though most of the examples in this book are drawn from food retailing (because the majority of my consulting practice is in this industry), this new way of marketing applies to all retailing and service sectors. For example, Gary Mead, owner of Mi Amore Pizza & Pasta, in Lompoc, California, has tripled his sales in the past three years using information gathered when customers use their special Mi Amore Supper Club card. (At the same time, his advertising costs, expressed as a percentage of sales, have dropped 75%.)

Some words about reading this book

While writing this book, I debated its title with various colleagues. *Customer Specific Marketing* is self-explanatory in that it draws attention to the new emphasis of marketing to individual customers rather than to the mass market. The alternative title considered was *Differentiated Marketing* which stresses the crucial offer characteristic of customer specific marketing—different offers for different customers. The second title is shorter and easier to say, but not as self-explanatory. As you can see, the first title was chosen. However, both terms are interchangeable and are used accordingly.

Obviously, in a book of this nature, there is constant reference to customers and retailers. But how should they be described? Men and women are both customers and retailers. Should I use *he, she,* or the term *he (she)* when describing either? For ease of reading, I chose to refer to a customer as *she,* as the majority of food customers are women, and to a retailer as *he,* using similar reasoning.

As some readers will be new to the subject, while others are masters, and some will want a blueprint with detailed numbers while others will just be seeking ideas, it was a challenge setting out the book to meet these diverse needs.

My solution was to design the book in a "soup to nuts" sequence, interspersing numbers and tables where they most logically fit. However, each chapter is written as a self-contained piece which allows you to read them in any sequence you find appropriate.

To assist you in deciding how to read the book, here is a brief sketch of what it covers:

Part I: Premise

This section sets out the basic argument for adopting customer specific marketing.

Chapter 1 sets the stage, ranging from how my mother-in-law taught me that retailers often reward the wrong behavior to how retail pioneers are starting to address this.

Chapter 2 spells out the two principles of *customer specific marketing—all customers are not equal and behavior follows rewards*—with some key implications.

Chapter 3 explains the two levels of customer differentiation and why it's in the second level where the great profit gains are made.

Chapter 4 argues that with customer information you can confidently determine your own future without reacting, in puppet-like fashion, to every competitor's move.

Part II: Economics

The purpose of this section is to quantify the principles and demonstrate that adopting customer specific marketing makes economic sense.

Chapter 5 is, to me, the most important in the book because it explains the underlying economic logic of *customer specific marketing* and other comparable expressions, such as loyalty marketing and relationship marketing.

Chapter 6 is "numbers"-focused for those who wish to learn, step-by-step, where the profit gains come from when you switch to *customer specific marketing*.

Part III: Practices

This is a fun section, full of ideas and practices of the leading differentiated marketers around the world.

Chapter 7 covers the ten major differentiation avenues—the 10 P's—being practiced today by retailers.

Part IV: Measurements

This section introduces you to the new measurements available with customer information and shows how this information will impact your company's organization structure.

Chapter 8 walks you through a series of detailed tables that will become your new retail compass.

Chapter 9 describes how we will reorganize our businesses around customers instead of products.

Part V: Implementation

The goal of this section is to assist in your transition to customer specific marketing.

Chapter 10 sets forth the key issues involved in getting started.

Chapter 11 gives some guidance in going the distance after the first six months.

Part VI: Validation

The intention of this final section is to validate what you have been reading.

Chapter 12 shares with you the actual experiences of leading practitioners, expressed from their individual perspectives. It's a fascinating chapter full of insights, practical tips and, most important, reassurance.

Chapter 13 offers a few closing thoughts.

I believe that customer specific marketing will become the norm in retailing during the coming decade. I hope that after reading this book you will agree.

Part I: Premise

This section sets out the basic argument for adopting *customer specific marketing.*

Chapter 1 sets the stage, ranging from how my mother-in-law taught me that retailers often reward the wrong behavior to how retail pioneers are starting to address this.

Chapter 2 spells out the two principles of *customer specific marketing—all customers are not equal* and *behavior follows rewards*—with some key implications.

Chapter 3 explains the two levels of customer differentiation and why it's in the second level where the great profit gains are made.

Chapter 4 argues that with customer information you can confidently determine your own future without reacting, in puppet-like fashion, to every competitor's move.

My mother-in-law was right again—as usual!

Retailers are always trying to gain new insights about their customers. So, several years ago, when my mother-in-law began to tell me about her recent food shopping experiences, my curiosity was immediately piqued.

Winnie Mikuszewski lives in the western part of Massachusetts where there is an abundance of competing food retailers within easy driving distance of her home. "On Monday," she recounted with obvious pride, "I went to Stop and Shop where I got $40 of groceries for only $20, using their double and triple coupon offers!! Then, on Wednesday I went to Edwards, that large discount store, and bought the bananas they were advertising as a below-cost special! On Friday or Saturday I did the balance of my shopping at Big Y, using my frequent-shopper card."

I smiled as she finished her story and told her: "Winnie, you are one of those customers I talk about when I say that retailers should *reward their right customers and fire the wrong ones!* And you're one of the ones who should be fired (by the first two chains)!"

Well, my mother-in-law didn't respond too positively to my observation and in her own special way, quietly told me so! It took several days for me to realize that I was wrong, and she was right, again—as usual! It's we retailers who are the muddle-headed ones—not the customers!

Lessons from my mother-in-law

I learned two extremely valuable lessons from this interaction with my mother-in-law. The first was that if retailers advertise items at crazy prices, customers are foolish not to take advantage of them! After all, when a manufacturer offers us retailers a really low price on one of his lines, we buy large quantities of it. Why shouldn't we expect the same behavior from customers?

The second lesson was even more telling. Both Stop and Shop and Edwards are successful, profitable chains. Who, then, subsidized my mother-in-law and others like her, who walked out of their stores with their below-cost purchases? Obviously, it must have been their regular, profitable customers—the economic backbone of these companies! Yet, the very opposite should be the norm— the occasional and convenience shoppers should be sub- sidizing the regular customers.

For years, retailers have argued that having regularly advertised, deeply discounted prices brings price-orient- ed customers into their stores but that, over time, these customers convert to regular, profitable customers.

Research done by the Retail Strategy Center Inc. based in Greenville, South Carolina, shows that this widely held belief is a myth! A handful of these cus- tomers do convert into "good" regular customers, but the majority actually defect within twelve months of their first shopping visit! I have yet to find a retailer anywhere in the world whose investment in this type of shopper has yielded an attractive return on investment!

To win in the future, we must *de-average* our cus- tomers, understand the dynamics and profitability of each customer segment and then market to each segment accordingly. From all of my research and consulting on three continents, this stands out like the Eiffel Tower— and it is now possible.

Today, leading practitioners of customer specific marketing, via the use of frequent-shopper cards, are learning more and more about the *actual* behavior of their customers and, based upon this knowledge, they are structuring different marketing offers to different customers. In the past these decisions were based on assumptions and marketing myths.

You don't have to be a large chain for success in this quest. Indeed, one of the most advanced and most profitable global practitioners of this new, fact-based marketing is a single store operator! In two years, his profits have tripled! The key to his success is, as my mother-in-law taught me, deciding who should subsidize whom, and then differentiating his offers accordingly.

The evils of average pricing

The averaging of prices and costs over all customers was one of the key characteristics of the mass marketing era from which we are now emerging. Several personal examples testify to its weakness as a competitive strategy in an age when technology readily permits price differentiation.

Two years ago, I was in Colorado when my dictaphone broke. I planned to be on the road for another ten days, so I asked my host to stop at an appropriate store on the way to our destination. We pulled into a large office supplies warehouse where I selected a $189 dictaphone. I was in luck—they were having a One Day Sale with 30% off everything in the store. So I received $57 off the regular price from a store I was never going to visit again! By giving across-the-board discounts they *wasted* the markdown they gave me—and every other customer that day who had not read the newspaper advertisement trumpeting their store-wide sale! I was an accidental winner as I had been prepared to pay full price for my dictaphone.

The losers that day were the regular customers! If the store had a customer identification system, it could have rewarded its better customers with even deeper price cuts, advising them by mail of a special private sale just for them, while the occasional and convenience shoppers, such as myself, would happily have paid full price, thereby subsidizing the deeper markdowns for these regular customers. This, in turn, would have encouraged even greater loyalty, sales, and profits among these better customers.

A few months later, I was in San Francisco for a conference. While casually strolling the streets of that beautiful city, I wandered into a book store and crossed to the business section, as I habitually do. Browsing the shelves, I found a book I had always wanted to read. At the cash register, I found to my surprise that my $22.50 book carried a 10% rebate! I saw no signs in the store stating that hard-cover books were discounted. I was prepared to pay full price for the book. Yet I finished up $2.25 better off in a store that, once again, I shall never revisit!

These are examples of the evils of average pricing. Regular customers are subsidizing the occasional shoppers. Instead, they should be rewarded for their loyalty with better values, while the transient, convenience shoppers should be charged full price.

Customer specific pricing
How, then, can retailers differentiate prices to their customers? How can they offer prices relative to the worth of each customer?

Three pioneers of *customer specific pricing* illustrate *some* of the options available to retailers today. The companies are MegaMarts, based in Oak Creek, Wisconsin; Ukrop's Super Markets Inc. located in Richmond, Virginia; and Food Lion Inc. headquartered in Salisbury, North Carolina.

MegaMarts

Immediately inside each MegaMarts store are several kiosks. A MegaMarts cardholder, upon entering, simply walks to one of the kiosks, swipes her card across a glass reader, and waits a brief period for a printout listing up to 24 items specially priced *just for her!* At the bottom of the list is a message that these special offers are available for only the next three hours! When the customer checks out, the cash register automatically reduces the prices on any of the kiosk offers made uniquely to her.

The special offers made to cardholders using the kiosk can be programmed in any way the retailer desires. Currently, MegaMarts' wholesaler, Roundy's Inc., is working with manufacturers to arrange special offers to customers based upon where the customer is in her purchase cycle of various products.

For example, if a customer usually buys toothpaste every six weeks, wouldn't it be nice if she received a special offer for toothpaste on the fifth week of that cycle? Similarly, if you are a regular customer of MegaMarts, wouldn't it be nice to know that they may sometimes express their appreciation by giving *you* even better, lower-priced offers than those given to an infrequent or convenience shopper?

Ukrop's

In 1987, Ukrop's, a high quality, 23-store chain, launched the first frequent shopping card program among North American food retailers. The program has evolved over the intervening years so that today this chain is one of the global leaders in customer specific marketing.

One special feature of the Ukrop's Valued Customer (UVC) Card Program is the monthly mailing of over 250,000 individually addressed, attractive newsletters to all active cardholders. Each newsletter includes coupons specifically tailored to that cardholder, based upon her individual purchase history! For example, if you have a cat, you are likely to receive offers for cat food, but not for dog food. In addition, the depth of the price reductions offered may vary according to how much you buy of the particular item *and also* how much you spend in total at Ukrop's!

Ukrop's described their approach to differentiated pricing in one of their monthly customer newsletters:

Our relationship has its advantages!

At Ukrop's, we want to say thanks for shopping with us in as many ways as possible. The UVC card gives us another opportunity to do that. When you use your card, we can create special offers based on what you buy, just for you. Some of the bonus coupons below will be for the exact items you buy. Others will be for new products we thought you might like to try. Keep using your card—and you'll see your savings grow!

Food Lion

After one month of sign-up publicity, Food Lion activated its MVP card on January 4, 1995, in all 1,039 of its stores! The principle of the program is both brilliant and simple. Around each store, the company identifies 400-500 items with an MVP bib-tag featuring a unique price offer. If an MVP card customer's total order is under $20, then *any MVP-tagged item in her shopping basket* is automatically reduced 5% at the checkout. If the total order is between $20 and $50, MVP-tagged items are reduced

8

10%, and if the total order exceeds $50, MVP-tagged items are cut 20% at the checkout!

In effect, Food Lion now has a four-tiered pricing program, ranging from full price for the occasional or convenience shopper (who doesn't care to apply for the MVP card) to 20% off selected items for its biggest spending customers. This first-of-its-kind price strategy fits in neatly with the company's long-time advertising slogan, "When we save, you save!"

Customer specific pricing is not really new

It is important to recognize that customer specific pricing is not a radical change for food retailing. Over ten years ago, the Catalina Marketing Corporation introduced to the industry *basket specific pricing* in which special price offers were made to customers based upon what they purchased in each transaction. For example, if you bought a certain brand of toothpaste, you received a Catalina price-off coupon for another of the same item or for one for a competing brand.

Catalina, with installations in over 10,000 stores worldwide, has developed into an information-based marketing powerhouse and now offers a special program for *customer specific pricing. Retail Direct* gives retailers the necessary tools to measure and manage customer relationships—data collection, data warehousing analysis and customer communication. The system collects and stores *household specific* purchase information and can deliver incentives and messages in-store via a small printer located at the point of scan.

For example, Dick's, a Platteville, Wisconsin-based food retailer, issues special gift certificates of varying amounts to different customers (based upon their purchase history in their Insider Savings Club), through their Catalina printers. This has enormous implications for the future because it allows a retailer to communicate, one-to-one, with each customer without the cost and delay of the postal system.

The bottom line

As these different approaches to individualized customer pricing suggest, a wide range of options now exist for retailers to practice customer specific pricing. Indeed, the options seem almost infinite now that at least one company offers a front-end system that allows a retailer to offer a different price on every different item in his store for every different customer!

2

The two principles of
Customer Specific Marketing

In the previous chapter we saw examples of how customer behavior is influenced by the rewards offered, and how some food retailers have introduced *customer specific pricing* because they see it as an advance over their previous *one price fits all* strategy.

The first chapter was presented as a "flesh and blood" lead-in to the two principles of customer specific marketing which will be discussed in depth in this chapter. These two principles are:

1) All customers are not equal.
2) Behavior follows rewards.

We shall discuss them in turn.

1) All customers are not equal.
Customers buy different items when they visit a store. They spend different amounts. Some customers visit regularly, some infrequently, and some just once. Some were in your store today; others last shopped with you months ago. Some come because of your advertised specials, some come because it's convenient, and others come because they prefer your total offering. Customers

are different, and they yield different profits—and losses. Let's see how different our customers really are.

A look at five customers

A food retailer in the United States has a customer profile similar to that shown in Table 2-1. In this table, the five customers' names each represent one-fifth of the customers in the database. The top quintile (20%) of customers, represented by Lucy Loyal, spends per week (SPW) about $53 with a gross profit of about 25%. Lucy's shopping life with us is over seventeen years. This means that Lucy Loyal will spend this year about $2,756 ($53 x 52 weeks = $2,756) in our stores, for an annual gross profit of about $689 ($2,756 x 25% = $689).

Table 2-1: Customer Profile

Customer Name	SPW ($)	GP (%)	Stay (Yrs.)	L/T GP($)
1 Lucy Loyal	53	25	17+	11,713
2 Russell Regular	27	22	10	3,089
3 Stuart Split	8	18	4	300
4 Sherry Cherry	3	16	2+	50
5 Carol Convenience	1	15	1.5	12

Stuart Split, representing the middle quintile of customers, spends about $8 per week (about $416 over the course of a year) with a gross profit percentage of 18%, yielding about $75 in annual gross profits.

Carol Convenience, representing the bottom quintile (comprising many convenience and occasional customers), spends over the course of 52 weeks, about $1 per week or about $52 in annual sales. With a gross profit percentage of 15%, this is about $8 in annual gross profit.

The other two customers, Russell Regular and Sherry Cherry, have results which fall in between those of the above three customers.

It becomes blindingly apparent that with a customer profile like this, charging the same price and offering equal benefits to all five customers not only doesn't make sense from an equity viewpoint, but also makes us extremely vulnerable! Any competitor with a better *offer-bundle*, in the form of a combination of lower prices and greater benefits aimed specifically at our Lucy Loyals, could steal these most profitable customers (whom we are currently over-charging to subsidize our Sherry Cherrys and Carol Conveniences).

Of course, this is what warehouse clubs have done over the past decade. They lured away a significant portion of the traditional retailer's best (high spending) customers by offering them the lowest prices on large item purchases. The warehouse clubs focused on the high spending, high profit segment and left the low spending, low profit customers with the traditional retailers. Unable to fight back because of their inability to differentiate their offers easily, traditional retailers suffered.

But the justification for differentiating becomes overwhelming when we consider how much in sales and gross profits each of the customers in Table 2-1 contribute *over their shopping lifetime.* Lucy Loyal regularly shops in our stores for over seventeen years; Stuart Split about four years; and Carol Convenience about one and a half years.

This means that Lucy Loyal, our typical top quintile customer, spends about $41,340 over her shopping lifetime with us, providing about $10,335 in life time gross profits (L/T GP). This compares to Stuart Split's $1,664 in lifetime sales and $300 in lifetime gross profits, and Carol Convenience's lifetime sales and profits of about $78 and $12, respectively.

What a dramatic difference in sales and gross profits from customers who, traditionally, have all been charged identical prices! What a great opportunity it presents to a retailer to reallocate his advertising and promotional markdown monies in favor of his Lucy Loyals and Russell Regulars, and away from his Sherry Cherrys and Carol Conveniences, now that he has the information and tools to do so!

Yet, as you know, the practice of many food retailers has been just the opposite, with priority given to the convenience shopper. For example, a Carol Convenience can walk into most food stores, buy the specials (some of which may be below cost), and then go through the express lane receiving priority service, while the big spending, high profit Lucy Loyals wait in lines two or three customers deep!

Why have we treated customers the same?

Why, then, in the past have we treated customers all the same and offered them merchandise at identical prices? The answer, quite simply, is because we didn't have a cost-effective system to make different offers to our different customers.

But that has now changed—because technology has given us new tools. And as Daniel Burrus, the author of *Technotrends*, reminds us, *"When the tools change, the rules change."*

Now that the tools of retailing have changed, so too must the rules. And *all customers are equal,* the dictum of the past five decades of mass marketing, is the first rule to change. It is replaced by its antithesis: *all customers are not equal!*

Differentiation is now accepted and expected

Customers have already accepted this new rule. They understand that customers are not equal and know that different deals for different customers make sense. In fact, because of their exposure to the proliferation of differentiated marketing practices already in our society (particularly in airlines, hotels and car rentals), customers not only accept it—but expect it.

Recently, one leading food retailer commissioned an external survey of its customers some months after introducing a frequent-shopper card. The company wanted to learn their customers' thoughts about his new program. Two of the typical responses were:

"Quite right! You should reward your main shoppers, because they spend more!"

"I spend over $3,000 a year here! You should reward us for all of this!"

This company's customers were telling them that not all customers are equal and that they have accepted its direct implication of differentiated pricing.

Scott Ukrop, Vice President of Marketing, Ukrop's Super Markets, Richmond, Virginia, tells us (in his speech in Chapter 12) of similar findings at his company. He said that:

Customers like to be treated like the individuals that they are. We were pleasantly surprised that our customers did not mind receiving different offers than those of their neighbors. This had been a major concern in our organization. Customers accepted the fact that the offers were based on their purchases.

Such comments should allay the fears of those retailers who have been taught from their very first day in retailing to treat every customer the same—regardless of their economic contribution to the company.

The bottom line—all customers are not equal

All customers are not equal. We must incorporate this fact in our business strategy by de-averaging our customers and our offers to them, both to recognize their diversity and to optimize our profitability. We should not hesitate to introduce differentiated marketing—it is already accepted and expected.

2) Behavior follows rewards.

Man is an economic animal in search of self importance. Thus, our behavior changes in response to the economic and "egonomic" (to use Faith Popcorn's apt expression) rewards around us. We respond to positive rewards and avoid negative rewards.

This is abundantly demonstrated in our children. We continually influence their behavior with a mix of positive ("If you do this, I'll let you stay up late!") and negative ("If you do that, you'll be grounded for a week!") rewards.

Consider how our own behavior is influenced by our desire to maximize our frequent-flyer miles total. We choose one airline over another. We accept longer lay-over times at airports to connect with our favorite air miles provider. We prefer our airline affinity credit card over the proprietary card when shopping at our local department store. We choose hotels and car rental companies that offer air miles on our preferred airline. And when we check in at airports, we take the initiative to ensure that our frequent-flyer number has been recorded. We don't wait to be asked—it's in our self interest to ensure that our number is recorded!

Or consider this. How many of us let our magazine subscriptions lapse because we know that we will be offered an unbelievable, last-ditch, low subscription price 6-12 weeks after the subscription has lapsed? We have figured out that we will be rewarded for not renewing our subscriptions on time and have altered our behavior accordingly.

General Nutrition Center Inc., a chain of mall-based health stores, offers a Gold Card for an annual fee of $15.00, entitling members to 20% off their total purchases on the day they sign up and on the first Tuesday of each month. Want to guess which day of the month is the busiest? It's the first Tuesday!

We are like Skinner's pigeons

B. F. Skinner, one of the twentieth century's giants in the behavioral school of psychology, devoted his life to understanding how human behavior can be modified by altering the mix and value of the rewards in our lives. Like most psychologists, his early work was with laboratory animals, where one of his most celebrated successes was teaching pigeons to play table tennis through a series of positive reinforcements!

After several years of studying changes in customer behavior (drawing on the information in various retailers' databases), I'm sad to relate that we human beings are really a lot like those pigeons! We respond very readily to the changes in the reward structures around us! Indeed, our behavior changes in direct proportion to the increases and decreases in the size of the rewards offered.

Let me illustrate:

• One caring retailer has a program which gives senior citizens 10% off any purchases they make on Mondays. When analyzing the customer database, we found that two-thirds (67%) of the senior citizens' weekly spending at that company now occurs on Mondays. This is five times the rate of the other customers, who spend only 13% of their weekly total on Mondays. *Behavior follows rewards.*

• One retailer offered a free turkey to customers spending an average of at least $50 a week in the two months prior to Thanksgiving. The result? The number of households spending over $50 per week skyrocketed 20% over the preceding year! *Behavior follows rewards.*

• When one retailer announced that all advertised specials would henceforth be available only to customers presenting their cards, the percentage of company transactions on the card jumped 8% that very week. *Behavior follows rewards.*

• Another retailer told his customers that 1% of their spending during the course of the year would be donated to the church of their choice. Result: the participating cardholders increased their annual spending more than 5%. *Behavior follows rewards.*

• One retailer introduced an employee discount program based on household spending. Both the number of employees using a card and their total spending jumped more than 20% over the previous year. *Behavior follows rewards.*

Reward the behavior you seek

Quite simply, if behavior follows rewards, then *we must reward the behavior we seek*—and not the opposite, as occurs too often. The promotional activity of department stores over the past forty years illustrates this well. With their one-day sales, weekend sales, week-long sales, end-of-season sales, and other similar promotions, they taught customers not to shop in their stores unless they were having a sale! In other words, they were rewarding customer promiscuity rather than long-term loyalty (which, we assume, is what they really desired). This contradictory behavior is called *the folly of rewarding behavior A when we really want behavior B!*

Applying the principle

Our first task as retailers in applying the principle that *behavior follows rewards* is to ask ourselves two questions:

1) What customer behavior are we currently rewarding?

2) What customer behavior do we wish to reward?

To assist in answering these questions, consider:

- Do we want customer *loyalty* or *promiscuity*?
- Do we want *better* or *more* customers?
- Do we want *high* or *low* spending customers?
- What is more important to us—increased *sales* or increased *profitability*?
- What changes in behavior are required to hold onto more of our *good* customers and lengthen their average *stay* with us?
- Of the behaviors we have chosen as our goals, *which are the most profitable ones to be rewarding*?

The bottom line—behavior follows rewards

The principle that *behavior follows rewards* isn't new, of course. It's as old as recorded history. However, what is new for retailers is that with a customer database we can make different offers to different customers, measure the changes in behavior, and then refine our offers accordingly.

As retailers, after we have set our corporate goals, we must review our existing customer reward structure and consider how it can be changed to better reward the customer behavior that moves us closer to our chosen goals. It's folly to do otherwise! *In essence, we must water what we want to grow. But first, we must decide what we want to grow!*

Achieving success

Like everything else in life, success is based upon the application of sound principles. The greater the application, the greater the success. Customer specific marketing is no different. The more you embrace customer specific marketing and base your business strategy on its two principles—*all customers are not equal* and *behavior follows rewards*—the better will be your results. In other words, to achieve great success, you must make customer specific marketing the core strategy.

Too many companies introduce frequent-shopper card programs and don't see any profit improvement. Usually, this is because they are just that—*programs*, and not a change in core strategy. To succeed with customer specific marketing, it must become central to your business—it cannot be an add-on to an existing marketing program. It means abandoning a host of existing marketing practices. It means focusing resources on the gathering of customer data so that you can make intelligent, differentiating decisions. *It means re-engineering your marketing strategy—indeed, ultimately, your whole organization.*

The other ingredient for success

Embracing customer specific marketing as your core strategy is the first ingredient for success. The second is the practice of *differentiation*. As all customers are not equal, it is logical that our offers should be different for different customers. The next chapter is devoted to this single idea.

3

The secrets of differentiation

It's important to understand that capturing the majority of your transactions and sales—even as high a share as 60% of customers' transactions (and over 80% of your sales)—on your card will not guarantee an improvement in profitability. *The big improvements in profitability come through differentiating your offers to different customers.* This means de-averaging your customers and offering better deals to some customers and lesser ones to others.

Retailers' margins are tight. We have only a certain amount of money to allocate to our two marketing costs: advertising and markdowns. We must make choices. It is logical that we should direct these marketing costs towards those customers we think will yield the greatest return—and away from those we think will yield the least return.

Differentiation means not trying to be all things to all people—but being some very clear things to certain people. This concept echoes Sol Price, the founder of Price Co., who stated that he believed in (and practiced) "the intelligent loss of business." Let's not forget, that includes the intelligent loss of customers!

This idea is heresy for many. It has proven the tallest hurdle for retailers contemplating customer specific marketing because it goes against the way we were trained. Yet it is logical, given our two primary principles.

My observation over the past three years has been that *the more a retailer moves away from average pricing towards differentiated pricing, the more his profits increase.* This occurs because he is moving closer to matching his costs with his revenues, and as we learned in Economics 101, the optimal profit position occurs when marginal costs equal marginal revenues. *Thus, the concept of differentiation is grounded in basic economics.*

Differentiation in practice

In Chapter 1 you were introduced to companies practicing various forms of customer specific pricing. Two additional examples from leading practitioners in the art of customer differentiation follow:

Do all customers receive the same offers?

No. The types of special offers you receive are based on your shopping. Quite simply, the more you shop at Green Hills, the better the offers will be. We want to reward our best customers!

- from a customer newsletter of Green Hills Farms, Syracuse, New York

You are special. One of our very best customers!

We really appreciate you! Your business means a great deal to us, and we intend to reward your loyalty. You have accumulated over 1000 points with your Club Greg card. That makes you one of our very best customers, and we want to give you special treatment.

This special mailing contains valuable certificates available only to Club Greg members of your status. These certificates are for super low prices on a variety of great items. This is just our way of saying "Thank You" for being a loyal customer.

- from a special customer mailing of Gregerson's Foods, Gadsden, Alabama

Why do companies such as Green Hills Farms and Gregerson's practice differentiation? Because it works! Or, as Willie Sutton said when asked why he robbed banks—"That's where the money is!!"

In April, 1994, Gregerson's Foods launched its Club Greg card. Listen to what "Greg" Gregerson, CEO, was saying eighteen months later, in December, 1995:

Our traditional advertising costs are down 50% from last year, our same-store sales are up 5%, and our gross profit is up over one full percentage point! Differentiated marketing works!

Differentiated marketing, another term for *customer specific marketing*, is the making of different offers to different customers based upon their different past, current or potential value. It has exploded as a marketing practice because of the computer's ability to collect, process, and analyze customer information. And differentiation will become more commonplace as computers develop into even more powerful, more sophisticated, faster, and cheaper tools.

The secrets of differentiation

Leading practitioners have discovered, through trial and success, certain rules that enhance the practice of customer differentiation. They are:

- **The big profit gains come at the second level of differentiation**

The first level of differentiation is offering prices and privileges to all customers who present the card when they shop. This is how frequent-shopper card programs began. They offered, in effect, a two-tiered pricing system. However, once 55-60% of transactions are card-based, around 80% of your sales are being captured. This means that you have now moved into another one-price-fits-all situation for the majority of your customers who provide the bulk of your sales, and another price level for customers who provide the other 20% of sales. With this first level of differentiation, however, your gross margin will have increased because you will no longer be giving markdowns on sales to non-cardholders. (Of course the real, but difficult to quantify, benefit at this stage is that you can now harvest customer information.)

When the majority of transactions are being captured on your card, you can move to the second level of differentiation. Here, different offers are made to different cardholders based upon the value of the relationship. This is the level where the significant profit gains are made. *The more companies increase the degree of differentiation at this second level, the more their profits increase.* The reason is that as our two marketing costs move more in line with customers' sales and profitability, the return on our marketing investment increases. (This is why de-averaging our customer base is so critical.)

To maximize the gains from differentiating our offers to cardholders, there are two additional steps:

1) Apply qualifying thresholds to receive rewards

As the pioneers in customer specific marketing have found, *the more you skew your rewards (both economic and egonomic) in favor of your bigger spending, more profitable customers, the greater your profitability.* Therefore, to avoid wasting monies being spent on the least profitable customers, thresholds are applied.

The application of thresholds is easy. For example, a customer receives a gift certificate once she has spent $1,000; the next one at $2,000, and a third at $3,000.

In the United Kingdom, Tesco, the country's largest food retailer, provides its ClubCard holders with a reward structure based on 1% of their purchases, but with certain qualifications. One is that *each* transaction has a qualifying threshold of £10.00. As about half of all UK food transactions are under £10.00, the program applies only to customers with the larger, more profitable transactions.

Thresholds can be used in every retail and service sector. While in a shopping center in New Zealand recently, I shopped at Barkers, a men's apparel chain with its own frequent-shopper card. To be eligible for the card, a customer must spend at least $100 in one transaction. That threshold acts as an indication of the customer's potential value as a customer. Cardholders receive a 10% discount off any purchase made at any Barkers store, including sale items. In addition, each month, cardholders are eligible to win one of eight monthly $250 wardrobe prizes for which they are automatically entered each time they shop at any Barkers store. They also receive special Club Barker merchandise offers not available to the general public.

One of my favorite threshold examples is the *self-select* threshold to join the Marriott Courtyard Club. The Courtyard charges $10 to join. But to those who join, the Courtyard mails two $10 "cash" coupons, used to reduce a member's final bill on two subsequent visits. (Coupon use is limited to one per visit.) Based upon their future travel plans, guests *self-select* whether membership is in their best interest. Obviously, one-time or highly infrequent guests will decide it's not in their best interests to lay out $10, whereas regular guests realize that joining is. The offer sorts the frequent from the infrequent guest. Once a guest becomes a member, other benefits accrue, with rewards based upon the number of nights spent at Courtyards nationwide.

The independent Flygfyren supermarket group in Sweden also has a self-select membership program. In exchange for a one-time membership fee, Flygfyren mails the new member a book of discount coupons, redeemable both in its stores and at other businesses and worth many times the amount of the application fee. Thereafter, members are entitled to a purchase rebate credit. Even though Flygfyren returns more value than the fee to its members, the purpose of the qualifying fee is to help Flygfyren learn at the outset which customers see themselves as long-term customers. This of course is extremely helpful when segmenting customers for targeted offers.

2) Make rewards proportional

Making rewards proportional to customer spending and profitability is a further but distinct refinement of thresholding. It simply means that the more a customer spends, the more she should receive, proportionally, in rewards. This is the same idea as in our progressive tax structure—the more we earn, the more we pay, proportionately!

The objective of proportional rewards is threefold:
1) to appeal in a cost-effective manner to our competitors' best customers (who are currently subsidizing their less profitable fellow-customers);
2) to reward and retain our own best customers; and
3) to provide an incentive to our other customers to spend more of their food dollars with us.

Flygfyren is an ardent believer in proportional rewards. It provides a rebate credit to cardholders every six months, calculated as follows:

Rebate calculation:

On spending up to 10,000 kronor ... 1%
plus
On spending between 10,001-15,000 kronor ... 2%

plus

On spending between 15,001-20,000 kronor   ... 3%

plus

On spending between 20,001- 25,000 kronor   ... 4%

plus

On spending over 25,000 kronor   ... 5%

Thus, a customer who spends 22,000 kronor in the half year is entitled to a credit of 430 kronor (or 1.95% of the previous six months' spending).

Of course, the Food Lion program described earlier is another excellent example of proportional threshold rewards.

- **Avoid caps**

In setting up differentiation programs, we should be careful to avoid *caps*, or *negative differentiation*, a practice currently seen in a number of gas companies' programs. These programs are structured so that their cardholders receive a rebate percentage based upon their annual purchases. However, they have imposed a $70 rebate cap. One busy executive who spends a great deal of time on the road recently told me: "I have had to get five or six gas cards. As soon as I hit the $70 limit on one, I put that in my drawer and start on the next. They apparently don't want my loyalty! Really, all they are doing is giving me a short-term purchase discount." These gas companies' programs, by *capping* their rewards, are deliberately encouraging their best customers to defect to competitors with similar programs! Then, they have to turn around and find new customers to replace these high-spending customers. One wonders if this is the behavior these gas companies really want to reward.

In a nutshell

If we accept the premise that not all customers are equal, then a marketing strategy based on customer differentiation is the inescapable conclusion. This chapter identifies how to differentiate successfully.

As even our best customers shop in competitors' stores, it's crucial that we strengthen our magnet of attraction. We cannot fight the battle on all fronts. We must focus on those customers whom we believe are most important to us; then we must differentiate our offering in a way that enriches that special relationship.

With differentiation we want to reward our regular customers. Therefore, we should be bold, clear and non-apologetic about this. Signs in stores advertising that they reward their best customers have, understandably, been well received.

The basic purpose of differentiation is to transfer our marketing dollars from customers who produce a negative or low return on our marketing investment to those with much more favorable returns.

Finally, differentiation does not mean that any customer can be treated discourteously—it simply means that customers should be treated equally courteously, but rewarded differently.

4

Think, and act, strategically

Too many retailers practice puppet strategies. They permit their competitors to jerk their strings, to dictate their marketing strategy. For example, when a competitor introduces double or triple coupons or a senior citizen's program, they do likewise. They monitor competitors' advertisements and agonize when they are eclipsed by a penny or two on a bananas or ground beef promotion. Rather than give their customers a different choice from their competitors, these companies are offering just an echo. They are but puppets, whose actions are determined by their competitors.

One contributing factor to this common business behavior is the lack of customer information. Without such information the retailer's eyes are focused on his total sales figure. He has no idea what impact his mimic responses are having on the sales and profitability of his individual customer segments—on his *loyal* customers, his *split* customers, his *occasional* and *promiscuous* customers, or his *new* customers. Or the impact these mimic responses have on the *churn and turn* of his customer base.

Fortunately, this is changing. Companies that understand their customer dynamics are switching from being puppets to being puppeteers because they are measuring—daily, in some cases—the impact and results of their differentiated marketing strategies.

Pulling their own strings

One food retailer, up against some of the toughest and finest competitors in this country, switched from puppet to puppeteer over a year ago. Its management team now controls its own strings because they measure the effect of each decision on their customers. Recently, I had the privilege of asking the three top executives of this company what they had learned since switching to customer specific marketing. Here's what they told me:

• "Now we don't mind telling customers the reason some of them get better deals than others. Today, when a customer approaches us on the store floor and asks why she didn't get a special offer like her neighbor and then goes on about how much she has shopped in the store, we quietly take her across to the PC at our service counter, scan her card and find out what her shopping history has been. Usually, we find there has been minimal activity, so we say, in a nice way, 'Well, ma'am, I'm sorry but it appears that you have not been using your card very much because there's only one entry here in the last four or five months.' The customer then usually becomes flustered and says, 'But I shop here a lot anyway!' So we quietly say, 'We really would like you to use your card so that we can give you these special offers we are making to our good customers. As you know, the more a customer spends with us, the better the offers become, and using your card is the only way we can know this.' And—this is something new for us—we don't then turn around and give her the deal, which we would have done before the introduction of our program. The bottom line is that we are no longer trying to be all things to all people and trying to satisfy all customers in all circumstances. Information is now an extremely powerful tool for us!"

• "We are no longer trying to take customers away from our major competitor. Our focus is to make money on the customers who are already shopping with us!"

• "We have overcome the fear of differentiating our customers."

• "Our good customers are no longer subsidizing our occasional shoppers. Rather, it's vice versa."

• "We no longer watch every competitor's ad every week." (The Vice President of Marketing said that every Sunday morning he used to rush down to get the morning papers to see all of his competitors' ads! He doesn't do that anymore.)

• "We've found that only the cherry pickers complained about our new rules, and then it was only a handful of them."

• "Our good customers love being appreciated!"

• "With such a program, a company can't continue offering an Every Day Low Price program, honoring competitors' coupons, meeting competitors' prices, having a Senior Citizens program, and so on. You must *focus* entirely on this new way of marketing!"

This company, now a global leader in the practice of differentiated marketing, has seen a remarkable improvement in its profitability and is now a dedicated practitioner of initiating and differentiating, rather than imitating. It no longer cedes control of its destiny to its larger competitors, despite its competitors' deeper pockets. These executives now confidently pull their own strings because their customer information has demonstrated that their differentiation strategy is paying off!

Information-based retailing

Just as the nature of military strategy is changing from brute power to information-based electronic weaponry, so, too, is the nature of retail strategy changing. Retailing, like war, is fast becoming an electronic battlefield! Customer information and customer knowledge are now part of our arsenal.

Does a retailer who knows who his customers are, how often they shop, how much they spend on each visit, and when they start—and stop—shopping with him, have an advantage over his competitors who are without this information? Of course he does! It's comparable to sailing at night without a compass. Quite simply, a retailer today sailing without a well-utilized customer database is headed for the shoals of second class performance or the depths of disaster!

Information provides enormous leverage. Our objective should be to lever our insights and knowledge more effectively than our competitors do. *The intelligent use of information is now a competitive advantage to those who use it to drive their businesses.*

Change the terms of engagement

One successful way to jump ahead in a stable or stagnant situation is to change the terms of engagement. Nelson defeated the French at Trafalgar when he surprised them by changing from traditional side-by-side naval warfare to cutting through their ships and blasting their unprotected bows and sterns. A great deal of military, and business, success has occurred as a result of changing the terms of engagement.

Even in the movies we see this vividly portrayed. One of my favorite examples is when Indiana Jones, in *The Raiders of the Lost Ark*, is confronted in a narrow Cairo street by an imposing black-hooded, scimitar-twirling thug! Things look bad for Indiana—really bad!

But after assessing the situation, Indy nonchalantly steps back, pulls a pistol from his belt and shoots his potential assailant. He changed the terms of engagement from what his opponent had in mind! *He changed the nature of the battle to suit his strengths.*

So, too, are the early practitioners of differentiated marketing changing the terms of engagement in their marketplaces. They are changing the nature of the battle to suit their new weaponry—customer information. And like Lord Nelson and Indiana Jones, they are experiencing decided success! Their advantage, of course, will not last forever. Their competitors will learn the power of this new form of marketing and adopt it for their own use. In the meantime, however, like the early possessors of gunpowder, their technological advantage is tipping the marketing balance of power in their favor. Their challenge, of course, is to sustain their newly gained advantage.

Hi-Lo operators are vulnerable

Over the past forty years, two primary pricing strategies have been prevalent among traditional retailers: High-Low, or Hi-Lo, pricing and Every Day Low Price, or EDLP, pricing. We are now witnessing the *third wave* of retail pricing—*customer specific pricing*—which is superior to the two traditional formats.

Consider the typical Hi-Lo retailer today with his large number of advertised and unadvertised specials requiring in some companies up to 1,500 price changes a week in each store! In addition, he often has 1,000-4,000 items reduced and listed as Temporary Price Reductions (TPR's), ranging from a few cents to a few dollars off regular price. In addition, he may offer discounts on all items in various categories, such as 40% off all greeting cards. For good measure, he may also offer double coupons and possibly honor, in true puppet style, his competitors' ad prices and coupons.

Apart from the high cost of operating this strategy (including advertising, markdowns, executives tied up in weekly meetings, store labor, and inventory overages), this Hi-Lo retailer gives the same special prices to anyone who walks into the store—his regular customer, his competitors' loyal customers, convenience shoppers who never even saw his newspaper ad, and one-time shoppers.

This traditional Hi-Lo operator is now highly vulnerable to a differentiated marketer who can, armed with customer knowledge, offer a superior price package, but only to regular, higher spending customers. This attracts profitable customers away from the Hi-Lo operator who, in turn, replaces the lost high-profit sales by increasing his advertising, thereby attracting more of the low-profit, promiscuous shoppers in the marketplace. This, in turn, causes margins and profits to decline further. At the same time, the differentiated marketer is reducing advertising costs because he now knows of the low profitability and loyalty of the promiscuous shoppers who are attracted, like moths, by the seductive flame of heavy print advertising.

EDLP operators are vulnerable, too

In contrast, an EDLP operator has lower operating costs than a Hi-Lo operator because he advertises less, has fewer specials, and, therefore, requires less labor. His point of difference is that he offers customers lower shelf prices every day.

Many EDLP operators have resisted the change to customer specific marketing. The two most common reasons offered have been, "We want to have the lowest prices for *all* of our customers," and "We don't want to add any costs or complexity to our business."

These arguments are no longer sound because:

• *The EDLP operator can't gather any detailed customer data.* Therefore, he can't learn his customer composition or its underlying dynamics. His decision-making is still based on assumptions and not on facts, which places him at a competitive disadvantage.

• *The EDLP operator charges his best and worst customers the same price.* Even if his cost level is significantly lower, he is vulnerable to a differentiated marketer because he is charging his $10,000 a year customer identical prices to that of his $100 a year customer; he is charging the same prices to the customer with an $80 transaction that he does to a customer with a much less profitable $8 transaction!

Thus, the differentiated marketer can target and win over the EDLP operator's best customers by offering, for example, a quarterly discount to high spending customers. Or the differentiated marketer can *straddle* the prices of the major image items of the EDLP operator by having a lower price for cardholders and a higher price for non-cardholders. This puts the EDLP operator in an awkward competitive position. If he responds by matching the cardholders' lower price, the move costs him more because some of the differentiated marketer's sales are to non-cardholders and carry a high gross profit. If the EDLP operator matches the higher price, he loses his price image. And by staying at his existing price, his price image is compromised.

• *The EDLP operator can be beaten on benefits.* Because he knows who his best customers are, the differentiated marketer can offer these highly profitable customers non-economic benefits and privileges (which he can't afford to give to all customers). Of course, the EDLP operator, without customer information, cannot respond in a cost-effective manner.

• *Differentiated marketing does not have to be complicated.* As described earlier, one leading EDLP operator, Food Lion, has already started moving to a differentiated marketing strategy. The company's tiered pricing strategy is simple and inexpensive to operate. Yet it provides a vehicle for the company to gather customer data and skew rewards in favor of their higher spending customers.

For these reasons, it seems inevitable that EDLP operators, like Hi-Lo operators, will be forced to move to differentiated marketing.

Think, and act, strategically

As blunt-spoken General George S. Patton once said: "The best way to neutralize a competitor's heartbeat is to change the rules of play." The practitioners of customer specific marketing are doing just that—by being puppeteers, not puppets!

As we conclude the first section of the book, it appears obvious that the question that all retailers today should be asking themselves is not *if*, but *when*, should they embrace customer specific marketing? When should they adopt this information-rich marketing approach which will allow them to truly think, and act, strategically?

Part II: Economics

The purpose of this section is to quantify the principles and demonstrate that adopting *customer specific marketing* makes economic sense.

Chapter 5 is, to me, the most important in the book because it explains the underlying economic logic of *customer specific marketing* and other comparable expressions, such as loyalty marketing and relationship marketing.

Chapter 6 is "numbers"-focused for those who wish to learn, step-by-step, where the profit gains come from when you switch to *customer specific marketing*.

It's really about economics— not loyalty!

This brief chapter is, to me, the most important in the book because it provides the economic rationale for differentiated marketing. It demonstrates why loyalty marketing is talked about so much currently—it's because the *economics* of loyal (ie, frequent) large spending customers is so compelling. Read on to find out why.

The single greatest profit opportunity today
The single greatest profit opportunity today is to stop averaging our prices across all customers! There is no such person as the average customer. Therefore, we are always over-pricing or under-pricing our merchandise. Prices should be set in relation to the cost structure of each customer segment.

Economics favor the bigger spender
Costs comprise fixed and variable components. Small transactions carry a higher cost per item than large transactions where the fixed costs are spread over more items.

In food retailing worldwide, the more a customer spends during a year, the larger her average basket size on each visit. Over the course of a year, US food retailers find that their top 20% of customers have an average basket size of around $35, the middle 20% have an average basket size of $17, and the bottom 20% have an average basket size of $9. In other words, the top 20% of customers throughout the course of a year have an average basket size about double that of the middle 20% and four times that of the bottom 20% group.

Therefore, when we apply our fixed and variable costs to transactions, our item cost structure is always lower on the larger transactions, ie, those of our highest spending customers.

This economic bias in favor of bigger spending customers increases as we delve into the numbers behind the numbers. For example, a correlation exists between a customer's total spending and the average selling price of her individual items. The average selling price per item of a food retailer's top 20% of customers is 20-35% higher than that of their lowest quintile.

This means that *per dollar of sales,* the best customers have about one-fifth to one-third fewer items for checkout staff to handle. This adds to the cost differences between high and low spending customers and highlights even further the perils of average pricing.

Compounding this disparity is yet another major finding. The greater a customer's spending over time (and therefore the larger the transaction size), the higher the customer's gross profit *percentage!* This occurs because as the transaction size increases, the proportion of higher margin, non-basic and non-special merchandise increases. High spending customers do buy low margin basics and specials; it's just that because these low margin items comprise a smaller share of the larger-sized transactions, the gross profit percentage is higher.

Do you pay everyone the same wages?

The inescapable conclusion is that charging the same price to each customer is as illogical as paying everyone, from chairman to carhop, the same hourly wage! Our salary policies are based upon the concept that the our wage and benefits package should vary in proportion to each employee's economic contribution to the firm. The same logic should also apply to our customer price and benefits package.

The reasons retailers have not introduced differentiated pricing over the past decades include:

- we did not know of these cost and profit differences;
- we had no easy way to calculate customer profitability; and
- we had no simple, speedy mechanism to implement customer specific pricing.

By charging the same price on the products we sell, regardless of the customers' transaction size or total spending with us over time, we earn disproportionately more on these larger transactions (our bigger spending customers), and disproportionately less on our smaller transactions (our lower spending customers). This simple fact is an open invitation to competitors, existing and potential, to target our more profitable customer segments.

As mentioned earlier, this is what the warehouse clubs have been doing over the past 10-15 years. Drawing from its nationwide Panel Diary data, A. C. Nielsen at the SRI Conference (July 25, 1994) showed that warehouse clubs have a 77% above-average share of the spending of households with five or more members and a 90% above-average share of households with incomes over $60,000 annually. By offering superior value to these two most profitable supermarket segments, the warehouse clubs have siphoned off an inordinate share of food retailers' profits.

This has occurred while food retailers have stood flat-footed, having neither the means to measure what has been happening to their customer base, nor the means to differentiate their customer offerings.

But now retailers are understanding their customer economics and changing their marketing strategy accordingly. And those retailers who elect not to change will become cannon fodder for those who do. The choice is simple—but stark!

Retailers who understand these underlying differences in their customer economics are achieving significant profit gains when they apply the lessons to their marketing strategy. In most cases, their actions have not triggered a competitive response because the gains came more from trading customers than from a significant sales increase! Their competitors had no idea what was going on! This is classic stealth marketing.

The three basic approaches

Differentiated retailers are achieving great profit gains using one or more of three basic approaches:

1) They are withdrawing their low and negative margin offers to unprofitable customers. This is being done either through minimum spending requirements or by reducing the significance and number of low and negative margin specials in their advertising.

2) They are switching their emphasis from item pricing to pricing based on total purchases. This is being achieved by cutting back significantly their deep-cut item pricing and instead are offering discounts varying with customers' spending behavior.

3) For their best customers, they are offering even more aggressive prices and adding egonomic benefits to their offer-bundle. These exclusive, stealth offers are usually made through the mail.

These actions have two major outcomes:

1) An effective increase in prices for customers with low and negative profitability. The convenience customers in this group continue to shop with the retailer but now contribute more towards their costs. Because their effective price level has been raised, they are paying a more appropriate price for their convenience. On the other hand, a number of price-sensitive customers recognize the changes as a price level increase and take their low and negative margin business to competitors. (Note that this sometimes results in a fall of the total weekly transaction counts.)

2) An effective decrease in prices for the higher margin customers. Existing customers recognize the better value they are now receiving and respond by increasing their total spending with the retailer. (It never ceases to amaze me how much more a retailer's best customers increase their spending when this occurs!) In addition, the new lower price structure for higher spending customers also attracts new, high spending customers from competitors. (Note that this increased spending usually more than offsets the sales losses of the defectors.)

The net impact on sales varies according to which combination of the three basic approaches is pursued. I have seen food retailers' sales increases range from low single digits to healthy double digits. But in all cases, with well-executed strategies, an excellent profit increase has occurred.

The real power of differentiated marketing

The real power of differentiated marketing is that we can gather customer information, understand our customer economics, and market to each customer segment in a much more intelligent manner than ever before. We can monitor our customer activity on a daily, weekly, or monthly basis, and keep tweaking the various elements of our strategy without our competitors knowing what changes are being made.

A card—or any other means of systematically gathering customer data—is the key to this door of opportunity and understanding. But neither the card nor technology is the reason for the successes described above—they are simply the *enablers* for differentiated marketing. The real change in corporate fortunes comes from understanding our customer economics.

The breakthrough results of customer specific marketing come neither from customer loyalty programs nor customer relationship marketing, two current popular marketing mantras. Giving priority to customer loyalty is extremely important, but we first must understand *why* we should give priority to customer loyalty—*economics!* Success comes from understanding the economics of de-averaging our customers. Only by rearranging our offer-bundle of economic and egonomic factors and skewing it in favor of our most loyal customers (our most profitable segment) away from our least loyal customers (our least profitable segment), do we optimize our profitability. *Great success comes from a marketing strategy based primarily on understanding customer economics—and only secondarily on customer loyalty.*

6

The profit paradox

The reason customer specific marketing has such a devoted following is that it can increase profits in a short time. This occurs primarily because of the gross inefficiencies of average pricing as described in the previous chapter.

Many food retailing pioneers of customer specific marketing have experienced increases in their profit before taxes to sales ratio of 0.50% to 1.00% within one to two years of embracing the program. As the average food retailer in the United States has a profit before taxes to sales ratio of less than 2.00%, this translates to a profit increase of 25-50%. (Some companies enjoy even greater gains.) Furthermore, the gain is not a one-year wonder that evaporates in the heat of competition the following year. It sustains and builds as the company becomes more adept at differentiated marketing.

Because these results are extraordinary, I am often asked how such gains are achieved. Primarily they are achieved through an increase in gross profits and a reduction in advertising costs without any drop in sales—which, you will recall, is how "Greg" Gregerson described his company's success in Chapter 3.

If you wish to walk through the detailed, step-by-step calculations, this chapter is for you. It describes two possible scenarios drawn from actual case histories.

Alternatively, if you are already convinced of the

profit potential that exists in de-averaging your cus-tomers (or if reading a lot of numbers make your eyes glaze over!) *there is no need to read any further!* Skip to the next chapter. This chapter was written for the hardened skeptics and the analytically inclined readers.

Any fool can increase sales 6.0%!

Any fool can increase sales 6.0%! Just buy space in the newspaper and advertise crazy prices. Your sales will rise—but your profits will drop.

The paradox of customer specific marketing is that sales and profits can both increase at the same time! Retailers I have observed who have made it their core strategy typically enjoyed 6.0% increase in their sales trend within the first three months and a greater per-centage increase in same-store profits within the first six months!

How does a food retailer achieve this paradoxical combination? Obviously, it's not accomplished by doing more of what has been done in the past! It comes about by re-engineering our marketing strategy. It comes from significantly changing some of our traditional practices.

One retailer's experience

To illustrate some of the issues involved, let's review one food retailer's experience. This company, in an extremely competitive market, launched its card pro-gram by making two significant changes. First, the com-pany aggressively priced about a quarter of its newspa-per ad items, but made them available only to card-holders. And second, in launch week, the chain convert-ed about one-third of its 3,000 store-wide, Temporary Price Reductions (TPR's) to cardholder specials. Without a card, a customer now paid the regular price on these items.

CSM Economics

Option A

Table 6 - 1

Projections PTW for first 12 months after introductory period

Note: PTW = Per Trading Week

	%	$				$
Projected Base Sales PTW (based on current trends)		100,000	K		= Prime CSM Gain (before costs) PTW	986
					as percentage of sales 0.93%	
+ Projected CSM Sales Gain	A 6.00	6,000	L=A*K		- Ongoing CSM Costs PTW	(400)
= Projected CSM Sales PTW		106,000	M=K+L			(.38%)
~Annualized Sales 5,512,000					= Prime CSM Contribution PTW	586
					as percentage of sales 0.55%	
Current GP %	B 21.00				x No. of Weeks to Annualize	52
x CSM Sales Gain =		1,260	N=B*L			
+ Increase in Overall GP %	C 0.10				= Prime Contribution Per Store (Annzd)	30,472
x Projected CSM Sales =		106	O=C*M		*as percentage of sales* 0.55%	
= CSM Gross Profit ($) Gain		1,366	P=N+O			
					- One-Time Introductory Costs per Store	(20,000)
Current Labor/Ben. %	D 10.50				= First-Year Contribution Per Store	10,472
Incremental Labor/Ben.%	E 8.00				*as percentage of sales* 0.19%	
~ Incremental Labor/Ben. Cost =	new 10.36	(480)	Q=E*L		x No. of Stores in Program	10
					~ Annualized Co. CSM Gain* (first year)	104,720
Current Traditional Advtg %	F 0.84					
Est. Reduction (as % of Sales)	G (0.10)				~ Annualized Coy. CSM Gain* (ongoing)	304,720
~ Advertising Savings	new 0.70	100	R=G*K		*before tax	
~ Prime CSM Gain PTW		986	S=P+Q+R			

CSM Economics — Option B

Table 6 - 2

Note: PTW = Per Trading Week

Projections PTW for first 12 months after introductory period

Item	%	$	Code	Item	%	$
Projected Base Sales PTW (based on current trends)		100,000	K	= Prime CSM Gain (before costs) PTW		1,340
				as percentage of sales	1.33%	
+ Projected CSM Sales Gain	A 1.00	1,000	L=A*K	- Ongoing CSM Costs PTW	(.40%)	(400)
= Projected CSM Sales PTW		101,000	M=K+L	= Prime CSM Contribution PTW		940
~Annualized Sales 5,252,000				*as percentage of sales*	0.93%	
Current GP %	B 21.00			x No. of Weeks to Annualize		52
x CSM Sales Gain =		210	N=B*L	= Prime Contribution Per Store (Annzd)		48,880
+ Increase in Overall GP %	C 1.00			*as percentage of sales*	0.93%	
x Projected CSM Sales =		1,010	O=C*M	- One-Time Introductory Costs per Store		(20,000)
= CSM Gross Profit ($) Gain		1,220	P=N+O	= First-Year Contribution Per Store		28,880
				as percentage of sales	0.55%	
Current Labor/Ben. %	D 10.50			x No. of Stores in Program		10
Incremental Labor/Ben.%	E 8.00			~ Annualized Co. CSM Gain* (first year)		288,800
~ Incremental Labor/Ben. Cost =	new 10.48	(80)	Q=E*L			
Current Traditional Advtg %	F 0.84			~ Annualized Coy. CSM Gain* (ongoing)		488,800
Est. Reduction (as % of Sales)	G (0.20)					
~ Advertising Savings	new 0.63	200	R=G*K			
~ Prime CSM Gain PTW		1,340	S=P+Q+R	*before tax		

With just these two straightforward changes, this company's same-store sales jumped 6% over trend (measured by comparing the year-to-year sales gains in the eight weeks after the launch to the eight weeks before the launch). In this particular case, half of the gain came from increased customer transactions, and the other half came from an increase in the average customer transaction.

Furthermore, gross profit, both as a percentage of sales and in dollar terms, increased. The gross profit percentage increase puzzled management, so we analyzed the causes. We found that despite the lower special prices offered, because they were available only to cardholders and because the number of items a cardholder could buy at that price on any one visit was limited, the off-take was not as high as for a previously advertised special. In addition, sales of the 1,000 TPR's to those customers who elected not to sign up for the free card were at full price, rather than at the temporarily reduced price, thereby yielding a higher gross profit percentage. Finally, the higher transaction size meant that a broader range of products was being purchased which, for reasons described in the previous chapter, also contributed to the gross profit percentage increase.

A year after the launch, the chairman called to tell me that gross profit was one full percentage point higher than in the previous year, and this was having a wonderful effect on the bottom line!

How the paradox works

Table 6-1, Customer Specific Marketing (CSM) Economics, illustrates how the paradox works. If you wish, key this table onto a spreadsheet and test various assumptions for a sense of what customer specific marketing might do for you. In doing this, keep in mind that-no one strategy is "best." The best strategy for you depends on whether you are first, second, third, or last in your market with this new marketing approach and on how you differentiate your offer-bundle from the other players.

For the sake of simplicity, assume that you are projecting a sales level of $100,000 *per trading week* (PTW) based upon a continuation of recent trends. (*Per trading week* is another expression for *per store per week.*) With the introduction of differentiated marketing and using approaches such as those mentioned above and elsewhere in this book, let's assume you achieve a sales increase over trend of 6% (see A in Table 6-1), or $6,000 per week, lifting your sales per trading week to $106,000.

Your gross profit increases

Despite being more aggressive with your pricing to cardholders, your overall gross profit percentage increases for two reasons: some customers don't become cardholders and therefore pay full price (giving you a full margin on their sales); and among cardholders, different markdowns are offered to different groups (as described in Chapter 1).

In the table the increase in gross profit is calculated in two steps: (1) your existing gross profit percentage of, say, 21.0%, is applied to the weekly sales increase of $6,000, yielding $1,260 of increased gross profit per trading week (see N in Table 6-1); and (2) your estimated increase in gross profit percentage on all sales as a result of the differentiated pricing of, say, 0.10% is applied to total sales, yielding $106 per trading week ($106,000 x 0.10% = $106). Combined, these two factors have increased your gross profit by $1,366 per trading week. (See P in Table 6-1.)

In the example, I have used a conservative gross profit percentage increase of just 0.10% to 21.10%. What this figure will be for your company depends on what differentiated pricing strategy you offer.

Labor increases

Of course, an increase in sales requires additional labor, but on an incremental basis. In the example in Table 6-1, a labor and benefits rate of 10.50% of sales is assumed. As this includes a number of fixed labor functions (such as opening and closing the store) that do not vary with changes in weekly sales, we need to charge only the incremental (or variable) labor costs against the $6,000 sales increase. (You can estimate your incremental labor costs by looking at your labor scheduling standards). In Table 6-1, an incremental rate of 8.00% has been assumed which, when applied to the sales gain of $6,000, increases labor costs by $480 per trading week. (See Q in Table 6-1.)

Advertising is cut

One fascinating discovery with differentiated marketing is that traditional print advertising can be cut with no noticeable adverse impact on sales! Both Gregerson's Foods in Gadsden, Alabama, and Ukrop's in Richmond, Virginia, have cut their newspaper and other print advertising at least in half. Meanwhile, others, such as Morgan's Tuckerbag, in Melbourne, Australia, Dorothy Lane Market in Dayton, Ohio, and Green Hills Farms, Syracuse, New York, have eliminated print advertising completely! This works because different customers are targeted with different offers, and newspapers and circulars are poorly suited to communicate these new variable, targeted offers. So, Table 6-1 assumes an extremely modest reduction in advertising costs of 0.10% of base sales, or $100 ($100,000 x 0.10% = $100) per trading week.

Prime gain
Based on this set of assumptions, a *prime gain* of $986 per trading week results. (See S in Table 6-1.) This comprises the gains from the increased gross profit ($1,366) and reduced advertising ($100), offset by the increase in labor and benefits ($480). This is the equivalent of 0.93% of store sales.

Other incremental costs
From this figure, however, we must deduct all other incremental costs associated with this new marketing approach. These are broken into two parts: ongoing additional costs and one-time transition costs.

The ongoing costs include such items as card costs and their issuance, software and hardware license and maintenance costs, the cost of employees hired for data analysis, and mailing costs to members (to the degree that they are not included in the advertising reduction above). These additional costs are converted to a cost per trading week and are deducted from the *prime gain*, resulting in the prime contribution on an ongoing basis.

In Table 6-1, we see that an ongoing incremental marketing cost of $400 per trading week (0.38% of sales) is assumed, which yields a *prime contribution* of $586 per trading week ($986-$400=$586). Multiply this figure by 52 to find the ongoing annualized gain of $30,472 ($586 x 52) per store. This amount in turn can be multiplied by the number of stores to yield a *profit contribution increase* on an ongoing basis of $304,720 ($30,472 x 10 stores).

The ongoing contribution
In this example, the *ongoing contribution gain* of $586 works out to be 0.55% of sales (before taxes) based upon the assumptions given. I have seen results a lot better—and a lot worse! I have seen much better gross profit improvements—and much higher cost increases! The

final results will reflect each company's execution of its new core strategy and the degree of its customer differentiation.

One-time costs and the net contribution

There is one other set of costs to consider. During the transition to customer specific marketing, a number of one-time costs (such as the launch costs) should be segregated from the ongoing costs and included in this caption. One-time costs can vary dramatically from company to company. For example, costs can be high for a company that does not have the latest technology in either cash registers or computers.

In Table 6-1, we have assumed a one-time cost per store of $20,000 so that the *net contribution gain* per store is $10,472 in the first year compared to $30,472 per store on a continuing basis.

The low sales growth alternative

As mentioned earlier, many options are available when converting to differentiated marketing. Some food retailers, to avoid prompting a strong competitive response, decide on a minimal sales/high profit approach by focusing on changing the customer mix. They plan to lose marginal customers and more than compensate with increases in sales and profits from their higher spending customers. This is usually accomplished by moving quickly and decisively to a Best Customer program, described later in Chapter 11.

The economics of this alternative are illustrated in Table 6-2. This example assumes a 1% sales increase, compared with the 6% increase in Table 6-1. However, based upon actual experiences of this approach, we assume that changing our customer mix in favor of our bigger spenders yields a gross profit hike of 1.00% (compared to the earlier 0.10%). The only other assumption changed from Table 6-1 is that advertising is cut by 0.20% rather than 0.10% of sales.

Comparison of the two scenarios

The difference in results between these two scenarios is dramatic. The second approach provides an *ongoing contribution gain* of 0.93% of sales compared to 0.55% in the earlier example. Keep in mind that the typical US food retailer has a profit before taxes to sales ratio of a little under 2.0%. Therefore, on an ongoing basis, the typical food retailer's profits would increase over 25% in the first example and over 45% in the second example. These are extremely attractive options in today's tough business climate!

Part III: Practices

This is a fun section, full of ideas and practices of the leading differentiated marketers around the world.

Chapter 7 covers the ten major differentiation avenues—the 10 P's—being practiced today by retailers.

New tools for your marketing toolbag

There are ten major avenues currently being explored by the leaders in customer specific marketing to heighten their customer differentiation. In concept, these are not new ideas. In reality, they are because of the ease, speed, specificity, and measurability that customer databases and computer processing power add to marketing today.

These ten dimensions—the 10 P's—are:

1) Price
2) Purchases
3) Points
4) Partners
5) Prizes
6) Pro Bono
7) Privileges
8) Personalization
9) Participation
10) Presto

Each stresses a distinct attribute and each resonates differently across the customer spectrum. Thus, each retailer must develop, from the above ten-point offer-bundle, that combination which best suits *his* customers, distinctly differentiates him from his competitors, and builds solidly upon his company's inherent strengths.

Obviously, no one offer-bundle is best for all competitive situations. You must craft, and then refine and change over time, that combination which is optimal for your company.

When developing your unique offer-bundle, first ask yourself: *What behavior am I seeking in our customers?* Then ask: *What combination of the 10 P's will best encourage this behavior?*

Although several of the dimensions overlap in definition, enough distinction exists to justify a separate classification.

Let's examine how each of the 10 P's are being practiced around the world today...

1) Price

Price has always been part of the traditional marketing mix. It is included in the new offer-bundle because it takes on a fresh complexion in an era when we no longer have "one price fits all."

Cardholder/non-cardholder differentiation

In general terms, the most basic form of price differentiation is between a cardholder and a non-cardholder. A retailer can offer lower prices to his regular, card-carrying customers while non-cardholders pay full price, thereby subsidizing regular customers' lower prices.

Simple price differentiation practices between cardholders and non-cardholders include:

Electronic price discounts. When a customer presents her card at the checkout and purchases any item with a lower cardholder price, the lower price is automatically recorded.

Multi-unit buys. When a cardholder buys a certain quantity of a product, she can purchase the next item at a lower price. For example, a cardholder may buy the first three items of a product for $1 each and the fourth for $0.10. Or a company may offer cardholders a number of items around the store with the tag line, "Buy three, get the fourth one free!" The purpose of multi-unit buys is, of course, to reward the larger spending customer, using threshold pricing. In this way, some retailers compete on a price-per-ounce basis against warehouse clubs. Obviously, multi-buys should typically be offered on items of which people buy two or more—it works better with soda than shoe polish!

Multi-product buys. These differ from multi-unit buys in that they offer cardholders a lower price on product-related items around the store. For example, if you buy both strawberries and whipped cream, the cream may be reduced $0.50.

Buy One, Get One Free (or Get Two Free!) This is a variation of the multi-buy program, but because of its cost, is not used often. However, when offered to cardholders, it typically generates a strong response. Some companies have also found the *buy one, get one free* approach an excellent way to introduce new products (both national brand and private label) to customers. Determining customers' acceptance of the new product is an easy step—measure the percentage of customers in the database who re-purchased the product. This information then contributes to the decision of whether to retain the new product. This is yet another illustration of the power of customer information.

Double Coupons. Rather than doubling or tripling coupons for anyone, some retailers *now* restrict this privilege to regular customers—their cardholders.

Customer Specific Pricing

Beyond the basic cardholder/non-cardholder differentiation set out above is *customer specific pricing.* Three approaches were described in the discussion of MegaMarts, Ukrop's, and Food Lion in the first chapter. Each of these companies is differentiating their prices among different customer segments based upon various purchasing criteria. They are achieving customer specific pricing using kiosks, targeted coupons and tiered-pricing, respectively.

Kiosks

A kiosk is, essentially, a personal computer with a box around it. Its power lies in how it is programmed. Spokane, Washington-based MEI (with its installation in MegaMarts) and Dallas, Texas-based Retail Services Inc. (with its installation in Farm Fresh, Virginia Beach, Virginia) are two of the current kiosk leaders in the food industry.

These companies understand that kiosks can be a potent deliverer of up-to-the second *customer specific pricing.* In addition, they realize the kiosk's ability to go beyond offering just prices to customers by offering other *customer specific benefits,* such as recipes, birthday greetings, and surprise gifts to customers as well. In addition, a kiosk can be programmed to show a cardholder her latest points or accumulated spending balances. Thus, a kiosk can be an excellent *customer specific communication device* thereby replacing a significant part, if not all, of a company's print advertising and direct mail.

To achieve these benefits however, a retailer must remember the second principle: *behavior follows rewards.* He must ensure each customer is rewarded for using the kiosk—she must receive great value when she swipes her card across the kiosk's reader. The more attractive the customer specific prices and offers in the kiosk are, the more customers will use it.

Straddle pricing

A differentiated marketer competing against a traditional retailer has a wonderful opportunity to gain a strong price image at a lower cost. This is achieved by selecting a number of the store's image items and increasing their regular shelf prices above those of the traditional competitor while reducing the cardholders' prices on the same items to below those of the competitor. This is called *straddle pricing.* In this case, if your competitor reduces his prices to equal your lower cardholder price, it will hurt him more than you, as all of the items he sells will be at the lower price, while you will be selling probably only 80-85% of your items at that price. The same approach can be used with your competitor's advertised specials. You can reduce your prices on his hottest advertised prices—but for cardholders only, of course!

What percentage of specials for cardholders?

What percentage of your specials should be available only for cardholders? This question is often asked by retailers contemplating differentiated marketing. Initially, it's a "chicken and egg" type question. You want to encourage customers to apply for and use the card. Therefore, the card must be attractive with many specials for cardholders. At the same time, you don't want to launch your program by saying to customers, "Yesterday you were able to buy all these items without a card, but this week you must have a card to buy our specials!"

One approach that works well in practice is to offer about 25% of the advertised specials on the card during launch week, and then increase this percentage to 80% or more over the next 8-10 weeks.

Then your future plan can be determined. Do you wish to have some specials in the store that shoppers can obtain without signing up for a card? The argument in favor of this approach is that it doesn't force every shopper to become a cardholder. In fact, it's probably not in your best interests for all shoppers to be cardholders because of the administrative costs involved in signing up one-time and infrequent shoppers.

Another argument against having 100% of your specials on the card is that this can give you negotiation leverage with manufacturers. One company, for example, has about 80% of its store specials available for cardholders. The other 20% are available to cardholders and non-cardholders alike. In this company's negotiations with manufacturers, after the parties agree on a price, the company then asks the manufacturers if they would like to include the item on the card program, which requires an additional price concession from the manufacturer. (One assumes, however, that manufacturers quickly learn of this approach and structure their offers accordingly!)

In practice, most differentiated marketers appear to be moving toward making all promotional prices across all departments available to cardholders only, as the value of the information and the incremental gross profit gained is considered greater than the disadvantages involved.

Limits

To allow deeper price cuts for regular customers, while at the same time preventing over-buying by a small (but very price-sensitive) segment of the customer base, some companies limit the number of items that can be purchased at the promotional price. This is really a form of rationing to allow a retailer to give greater value to a broader range of regular customers. Some companies, such as Springfield, Massachusetts-based Big Y, limit all cardholder specials to five—no exceptions, not even when they have one of their famous *Buy One, Get Two Free* promotions when cardholders are able to buy, for example, 5 dozen eggs and receive 10 dozen free!

Other retailers place limits on only some of their specially priced items, or set varying limits on selected items, while yet others offer time-based limits such as, "Each cardholder may buy up to four dozen cases of Coca-Cola at this special price at any time during the week." In this latter case, the system is programmed to ensure that the special prices offered are not available beyond those limits for each individual cardholder!

Of course, from a customer's perspective, either a standard limit on all items, as at Big Y, or no limits at all would be simplest. Varying limits on items can be irksome and therefore should be avoided.

Whether purchase limits should be imposed at all depends on whether an aggressive differentiated pricing program is in place. For example, if in addition to advertised specials, a monthly mailer is sent to your best customers offering the advertised items at even lower prices, limits seem inappropriate and confusing.

As computer power is further enhanced, customer management programs are developed, and retailers introduce direct customer profitability, *customer specific pricing* will become commonplace, and we can expect many new pricing approaches to emerge.

Limitations of price

A price focused strategy has one major limitation. Its reward structure is based on individual products. Promoting and rewarding their purchase is the *indirect* way to achieve the desired customer behavior a retailer really wants (which, one assumes, is frequent, high spending customer visits). A price-focused approach does not always achieve that result. The disciples of B. F. Skinner would argue, "If you really want high spending regular customers, why don't you just directly reward such specific behavior?" That's what the following section is all about.

2) Purchases

While having special cardholder prices on selected products around the store has been a food retailer's typical entry point into differentiated marketing, some companies are now regularly offering their cardholders price concessions on certain products based upon how much they purchase over a specified period. (These offers are in addition to the other special cardholder prices around the store.) The objective of this practice is to give an even greater price advantage to the regular, higher spending customer.

Since our goal as retailers is to have more higher spending customers, this is rewarding the behavior we desire. Some airlines, such as British Airways and Qantas, have already moved in this direction by biasing their reward structure in favor of how much you spend (on tickets) rather than on the miles flown. They obviously prefer revenues to mileage!

Item purchase rewards

Cardholder price concessions on certain products, based upon the amount purchased over a specified period, are best illustrated by the free turkey offers at Thanksgiving in recent years. A number of retailers have been offering their cardholders a free turkey if they achieved a pre-determined purchase threshold in the 6-10 weeks prior to Thanksgiving. For example, spend $400 in the eight weeks prior to Thanksgiving, and receive a free turkey. Then, to avoid depreciating the value of this offer, the company does not advertise or promote turkeys during Thanksgiving week. Instead, turkeys are offered in the meat cases at full price, despite traditional competitors running advertisements offering turkeys below cost to anyone who walks through their doors.

These free turkey programs epitomize the difference between mass marketing and customer specific marketing. The traditional retailer gives the same crazy low price to anyone in the marketplace. The differentiated marketer gives an even better deal—a free turkey—but only to his better customers. By announcing the turkey program to all customers in September, each customer *self-selects* whether she wishes to participate. By being loyal with her spending during the specified period, she can receive a free turkey. However, it forces a promiscuous customer to decide whether she will change her behavior over the next eight weeks. If she doesn't, she obviously will not qualify for the reward, and she will have to go to the traditional retailer to buy his below-cost offering in Thanksgiving week.

Now, the traditional retailer *hopes* that the shopper will buy a lot of other items to offset his turkey loss.

Some will. Some won't. The differentiated marketer, on the other hand, *knows* in advance that the free turkey customer is profitable! And he knows *which* customers increased their spending and what gross profits they contributed. In contrast, his traditional competitor is groping in the dark when it comes to understanding what the impact of this, or any other program he offers to his individual customers, is. Pure and simple, it's a one-sided battle.

Subsequent refinements to the turkey program have included offering a free turkey breast to any customer who spends, say, half the qualifying amount, and a full Thanksgiving dinner to those who spend double the amount. By offering a *range* of threshold rewards, all customers have an incentive to spend more of their food budget with the differentiated marketer.

Two variations of the turkey program that I've seen include a free Easter Ham program along similar lines and a *Christmas in July* program. In the latter case, customers are offered different levels of gift certificates depending upon the amount spent during July. For example, spend $200 and receive a $5 gift certificate; spend $400 and the certificate value increases to $15, and so on.

Periodic purchase rewards

A second example of a purchase reward offers a *percentage off your next purchase* gift certificate based upon purchases in each calendar quarter. For example, spend $250 in the quarter and receive a *5% off your next purchase* gift certificate; spend $500 or more in the quarter and receive a gift certificate for 10% off your next purchase. As such offers can be expensive, they are usually funded by withdrawing a number of the weekly specials or by offering shallower discounts on them.

The ultimate positioning of this second approach is the store with no specials at all, offering such purchase gift certificates with discount percentages increasing in proportion to the amount of the customer's total spending. This approach would truly reward a retailer's biggest spending customers and minimize the amount spent on his promiscuous shoppers. It puts the decision of what is "on special" back into the customer's hands. This approach is very customer oriented, for in deciding how and when to apply the gift certificate, the customer buys items when *she* needs them and not when the manufacturer or retailer wants to move them.

Rewarding customers proportionately more for higher total spending rather than for buying specific individual items is at the heart of rewarding the behavior you seek. It has proven very attractive to customers because *they* decide the size of their discount by the amount of their purchase. It's a potent new differentiator—not only does it make competitive response difficult, but also its simplicity reduces store labor costs.

For everyday low price operators, purchase rewards would be a logical entry vehicle into differentiated marketing. For the pure EDLP operator, this approach would instantly reward his bigger, more profitable shoppers and provide a strong incentive for customers to drive past competitors. With the value of the discount certificate increasing in proportion to the amount spent, the program also acts as a *defection barrier* to customers tempted to switch to competitors. The possibility of achieving the next higher discount percentage by spending more shopping dollars at your store is a strong incentive to remain loyal!

One side benefit of purchase rewards is that they induce customers to present their cards on every shopping visit, because all dollars, large and small, accumulate towards achieving the next threshold level. This provides you with a very rich activity profile.

Purchase discounts can be issued quarterly, bi-annually, annually, whenever certain thresholds are met, or even at the customer's discretion.

The Spend & Save card issued by Homebase, a major home improvement chain in the United Kingdom, shows how one retailer successfully uses purchase rewards. The program works on a rolling twelve-month basis and offers a series of threshold rewards. The first £100 of customer spending triggers a £4 gift voucher, as does each of the next two £100 cumulative levels of spending. The fourth £100 of spending triggers a £6 gift voucher, while the fifth £100 of spending triggers an £8 gift voucher. The sixth and any subsequent £100 of spending trigger a further £10 gift voucher.

Thus, if a customer spends £300 in a twelve-month period, she receives £12 in gift vouchers, but if she spends £600—double that amount—her gift certificates triple to £36!

Homebase cardholders receive a statement four times a year showing their spending to date. However, the first statement is not issued until a customer has reached a spending threshold of £100. And subsequent statements are issued only if cardholders are receiving notification of Gift Voucher rewards.

New Competitors

Purchase programs have been a powerful magnet to combat a new competitor entering a market area. By introducing a 6-, 12-, or 17-week purchase program with proportional rewards, the existing retailer provides his customer with an economic rationale to keep shopping with him. They may go and visit the new competitor and spend some money there, but having already built up some credit on their purchase program at their existing retailer, they are less inclined to switch to the new retailer.

Conversely, a purchase rewards program can act as an excellent Grand Opening gambit for a new entrant in the marketplace. A generous purchase program rewarding customers in proportion to their spending is probably of greater long-term economic benefit to the entrant than page after page of *grand opening specials* which primarily attract the area's cherry pickers.

Other applications of purchase rewards

Purchase rewards have been used very effectively by both General Motors and Ford with their affinity credit cards. In both of these cases, 5% of the purchases charged to their respective cards can be applied as a discount on the consumer's next GM or Ford vehicle, either purchased or leased. Charge $20,000 over a four- or five-year period on your GM or Ford credit card, and when buying a new GM or Ford vehicle, after negotiating the deal, a further $1,000 is subtracted from the price simply because of the $20,000 charged on the credit card.

Both cards, launched in recent years, have achieved great membership success. Obviously, this type of reward has great appeal. It is simple and meaningful. However, they are both currently structured more as purchase discounts than as loyalty cards, because both cap the annual discount their cardholders can receive.

For example, Ford has an discount cap of $700 that cardholders may earn each year. This obviously encourages Ford's best cardholders (its potential Jaguar buyers?) to switch to another affinity card, such as one offering air miles, once they have spent $14,000 during the year (5% of $14,000 is $700).

One interesting feature of both these cards is that they are *self-selecting*. Unless you plan to buy or lease a

GM or Ford vehicle, you'll not apply for their cards. Neither company is trying to be all things to all people. Their objective is to give additional value to the potential purchasers of their cars and pull back from their traditional price-oriented, promotional frenzies.

One very creative mutation of the GM-Ford credit card program was launched in mid-1995, and was scheduled to run for one year. Davis Supermarkets, based in Greensburg, Pennsylvania, sent a flyer to the area's residents announcing that members of the Davis Key Card program could earn up to $750 off the purchase of any vehicle purchased from any Smail Automobile Dealership, also based in Greensburg. Smail outlets offer a wide range of vehicles: Pontiac, Cadillac, GMC Truck, Isuzu, Honda, Lincoln-Mercury, Mazda, Mercedes Benz, Acura, and Mitsubishi.

The program was extremely customer friendly. For Davis Key Card members, 10% of each purchase was automatically added to the cumulative auto credit shown at the bottom of each register tape. When a cardholder wanted to purchase a car, she took her latest register tape to the Customer Service desk in any Davis store where it was exchanged for a Smail discount certificate in the amount of the accumulated credit. Then after the customer negotiated her purchase price with Smail, she presented her Davis discount certificate as part of the payment for the car or truck. For customers with, say, a GM credit card, this program would have been particularly attractive, as their Davis/Smail credit would have been in addition to any credit on the GM credit card.

In this example, a Purchase program was combined with a Partners program to enhance the value of shopping at Davis Supermarkets. And even though the Smail auto discount was capped at $750, it is unlikely that anyone would stop using their card once they had spent

$7,500 during the twelve-month period because of the many other special prices and benefits available to Davis Key Cardholders.

Disadvantages

The disadvantage of a purchase program can be its cost. To make it attractive, the rewards have to be high. To minimize the total marketing cost, rewards should be skewed heavily in favor of the higher spending (more profitable) customer. A retailer who selects purchase rewards as his primary point of difference should have fewer specials and apply the savings toward the purchase program. It's a matter of skewing your promotional and markdown program towards your primary point of difference in the marketplace.

3) Points

Airline frequent-flyer programs are the most widely recognized points program in existence today. Not only do airlines, hotels, and car rental companies use air miles as rewards, but also many companies, ranging from jewelry stores to mattress companies, are adding air miles to their offer-bundle. And just like the explosion of air miles as a reward mechanism, so, too, in retailing will the use of points programs explode.

Despite the great success of airline frequent-flyer programs and of points programs at merchants such as Dallas, Texas-based Neiman-Marcus with its InCircle program and Canada-based Zellers, with its Club Z program, very few US food retailers have shown much interest in points programs. This is now changing, as the versatility and flexibility of points programs are beginning to be recognized as very potent competitive weapons.

The many advantages of points

The use of points as the basis of your reward system has the following advantages:

• *Simplicity.* Points are a very simple way to allow both thresholding and proportional rewards, thereby skewing rewards in favor of your better customers. Points permit you to differentiate customers easily based on transaction size, shopping frequency, or accumulated spending.

• *Targeting groups.* Points also permit easy targeting of selected customer groups for certain periods of time, allowing measurement of the impact of any promotional program. For example, the top 20% of your customers could be offered double points for the last three months of the year or restaurants could be offered double points on any wine purchases they make in your stores.

• *Targeting departments.* Points can be used for targeting certain departments. Typically, points programs are based upon total spending, but they can also be used for limited periods for specific items or categories in the store. When I was visiting a Flygfyren store in Sweden, for example, they were offering 10% bonus points on any children's apparel purchased that month. In Morgan's Tuckerbag stores in Australia, double points are offered on produce purchases on Tuesdays.

• *Price image.* Rather than deeply reducing prices on advertised merchandise, heavy bonus points can be offered on those items. This type of approach may be particularly helpful to an upscale retailer who does not want to destroy his price image.

• *Price alternative.* Delhaize "Le Lion", one of Belgium's leading retailers, offers the majority of its weekly specials in the form of points rather than price reductions. For example, instead of reducing the price of coffee 50 francs, they may offer 50 points with each coffee purchase. This means, in effect, that the one-time shopper gets very little in the form of price reductions.

- *Avoid price wars.* Points allow you to give greater value to your customers without precipitating a price war with your competitors. This can be done, for example, by meeting your competitor's item pricing on selected items but then offering, in addition, points on these same items, which acts as a tie-breaker. Alternatively, your prices could be $0.01-$0.10 higher than those of your toughest price competitor but accompanied by the equivalent of $0.05-$0.20 worth of points to customers buying any of those items. This makes it extremely difficult for the competitor to outbid you because you have changed the rules of engagement.

- *Encourage multiple purchases.* Points can be used to encourage multiple purchases of items. For example, buy three or more items of any house brand and receive 100 extra points.

- *Build incremental sales.* Points can be used to build incremental sales by offering customers bonus points for all purchases in a quarter, based on how much they spent in the preceding quarter. For example, spend at least $250 in any quarter and receive 50% bonus points on all purchases in the following quarter. Spend at least $500 in any quarter and receive 100% bonus points on all purchases in the subsequent quarter. This not only acts as an inducement to increase purchases, but it also acts as a long-term hook to customers to return to take advantage of the bonus points.

- *Enhance school-funds programs.* Points can be used effectively for school fund-raising programs. For example, Big Y, the Springfield, Massachusetts-based supermarket chain, has run several very successful points-for-schools programs by identifying a number of items around the store which carry points that can be awarded to the school of the cardholder's choice. These points have a monetary value and are used by the schools for buying computers and other school requirements. The attractiveness of points in a situation like this is that they can vary significantly from item to item, depending upon the respective contributions of the manufacturer and the retailer, as opposed to the typical tapes-for-schools program which simply yields a percentage of each customer's total spending. The points approach is much more flexible. It also allows the retailer to offer generous points for schools on items around the store which are slow movers or deletion candidates. In this way, instead of markdowns being given to a customer, they are, in effect, given to the school of the customer's choice.

• *Special rewards.* Points can be used as a reward for cardholders who attend special event evenings or functions. In addition, customers attending such functions can be offered bonus points, rather than price reductions, on anything they purchase.

• *Promote quality control.* Points can even be used as an element in your quality control program. Several years ago, customers at Superquinn in Dublin, Ireland, were offered 100 SuperClub points if they encountered one of fifteen problems, such as finding an outdated item on the shelves or discovering a wobbly or squeaky wheel on their shopping cart!

• *Employee rewards.* Points can be used as an employee reward. Morgan's Tuckerbag in Melbourne, Australia replaced its 5% employee cash discount with double points on employee purchases. Besides being very well received, the program benefits the company because the employees' experiences with it makes them very knowledgeable when answering customers' questions about the program.

• *Unlimited flexibility.* The redemption of points can be handled with unlimited flexibility, ranging from cash gift certificates which may be applied against future purchases, as at Save-On-Foods in Vancouver, Canada, to a gift showcase at the front of each store, as Morgan's Tuckerbag offers, or to an extensive catalog of items, as Superquinn offers SuperClub members. Rewards can extend to air miles, discounted or free travel, ski lift tickets, and special events, such as wine trips. Also, there is no reason why retailers can't copy the practice of some airlines which invite cardholders with high points balances to bid points for unique events such as trips to France or the Super Bowl, or flying the airline's flight simulator. In addition, as at Morgan's Tuckerbag, customers can be invited to donate some of their points to a charity of their choice.

• *Build partnerships.* A points program is an excellent vehicle to build partnerships with other businesses because it allows cardholders to accumulate points at a faster rate.

• *Defection prevention.* Points act as a defection barrier. As customers build up accumulated points balances, they move towards higher thresholds with even more attractive rewards and therefore are less inclined to shop at competitors or to abandon you.

• *Revenue generator.* Points can even act as a revenue generator to a company offering its rewards through a catalog. Outside companies are often keen to advertise in the catalog, knowing that it has high readership.

• *Differentiator.* A points program can be a very powerful differentiator for a retailer, provided reasonable price parity is maintained with one's competitors. One highly successful retailer with a points program actually showed comparison shopping baskets at the front of its stores to reassure customers that the introduction of the points program did not cause any increase in prices. The points were seen as an added benefit, as a tie-breaker, which competitors could not match.

• *Encourage card-carrying.* A points program also acts as a wonderful memory-jogger for a customer to carry her card because every purchase moves her closer to her next reward threshold.

• *Other attractive features.* Finally, from a retailer's perspective, a points program has two extremely attractive features. First, it is an excellent way to skew rewards in favor of bigger spending customers by using a steeply inclined proportional rewards structure. Second, a points redemption offering which is highly proportional in nature encourages customers to delay redeeming their points, thereby building a permanent cash float equal in value to the unredeemed points.

Disadvantages

Even with these advantages, like every program, a points rewards system has its vulnerabilities and weaknesses. In particular:

• *Slow start.* A points program starts slowly. Until a customer reaches her first threshold level, the program is a delayed reward, rather than one of instant gratification. Thus it is vulnerable to aggressive competitive reaction in its early days when customers are building up their points balances.

• *Expensive.* If points are credited for every dollar of purchases, it can be an expensive proposition. For example, offering customers one point per dollar spent with each point equivalent to one cent costs just under one percent of sales (after allowing for non-redemptions). This means that a food retailer needs a significant sales increase to justify such a large cost increase. This is yet another reason for proportional rewards, rather than a flat reward. (One food retailer deftly side-stepped this high cost issue by awarding points only on selected items and not on a customer's total spending.)

- *Catalog undercutting.* Redemption items in a catalog, typically published for a 6-12 month period, can be undercut in value by another points program. A competitor could take identical items and offer them at a lower points redemption value. For example, one retailer was offering a brand-name toaster for 1,000 points; his competitor introduced a similar points program and offered the same toaster for only 800 points.
- *Points liability.* The liability for unredeemed points can escalate and cause concern to your financial executives. (Fortunately, this problem can be avoided in three ways: automatically issue points certificates when cardholders reach, say, 1,000 points; build up a cash reserve equal to the value of the outstanding points balance; or include a rule that the points balance in any account that is inactive for a full calendar year automatically expires.)
- *Complexity.* Accounting for points can be complicated. For example, if the produce department offers 100 points with each watermelon purchase, a charge for those points has to be made so that the department knows its true weekly profitability. Therefore, a standardized internal charge-out system for points is required.
- *Increased administration.* Administration of a points program can be more expensive than other options. One additional cost, for example, is customers calling for their latest points balance. Therefore, an easy mechanism for customers to check their points balance at any time is required: either an inquiry kiosk in your stores or an automated telephone inquiry system allowing cus-

tomers to call, key in their membership number, and automatically receive their latest points balance.

Points are flexible, appealing and exciting. A points program can truly differentiate your company in the marketplace. But again, to be highly successful with such a program you must leverage its unique attributes and make it the dominant feature of your offer-bundle.

4) Partners

Adding partners to the offer-bundle is one of the big growth areas in differentiated marketing today. Its great attraction is that it adds benefits to cardholders at minimal cost to the retailer.

Partnership programs can be particularly powerful when built on top of a points program, although this is not a necessary prerequisite.

One immediate advantage of a partners program is that it allows for an *omnibus card*—a single card which activates rewards at a number of different businesses. With the number of card-based programs proliferating, replacing many cards with one is very attractive to customers.

Partner programs range from simple to sophisticated and work successfully for retailers of all sizes.

Green Hills Farms

Green Hills Farms is a highly successful, single-store food retailer in Syracuse, New York. According to John Mahar, Director of Marketing, they have a long-term arrangement with a local car wash, a hairdresser, a gas station, and a dry cleaner. Anyone presenting a Green

Hills Farms card at the car wash receives an $11 deluxe car wash for only $5! Similarly, at the hairdresser, anyone presenting the Green Hills Farm Card receives 10% off the cost of his or her appointment.

From time to time, Green Hills Farms introduces limited-period partners. During a recent three-month period, Green Hills Farms cardholders were offered a 1% interest rate reduction on new auto, home improvement, personal and secured loans at a local bank. Reducing a customer's annual interest rate from 9.0% to 8.0% on a loan was very appealing to cardholders.

The nature of Green Hills Farms' relationship with its partners is that they give added benefits to cardholders, while Green Hills Farms gives free publicity about the partners to its cardholders. Everybody wins, and it adds yet another layer of value to the card.

Farmer Jack

A similar program in a much larger company has been carried out by Detroit, Michigan-based Farmer Jack. Farmer Jack cardholders, simply by presenting their card at Crowley's, a local department store chain, received a $5 Crowley Bonus Savings certificate with every $50 of regularly priced merchandise at the department store. At Fetter, a consumer electronics chain, cardholders received Farmer Jack food certificates for as much as $170 when they purchased various popular items in Fetter's stores. Fetter even carried application forms for Farmer Jack's card so that Fetter customers could take advantage of the great deals available.

Mobil's Premier Points

Partner programs can be narrow or specialized in their relationship. For example, Mobil in the United Kingdom has been using the Argos Premier Points loyalty program for a number of years. The card is free, and cardholders have it swiped whenever they purchase petrol and sundries at any Mobil station. The card accumulates points based on the amount spent. Premier Points are also available on the same card from various non-competing outlets, giving cardholders the opportunity to build points quickly.

Points can be redeemed for discounts on any item at any Argos catalog store throughout the United Kingdom. There is no cap; items can be paid for in full using the Mobil points.

The benefit of the program to Mobil is that it provides added value to its customers without starting a price war with competitors. Argos benefits because it opens up a whole new group of customers who now have a reason to shop with them.

Gatwick Airport's Bonus Points

Even members of shopping centers have banded together as partners and offered points on a card to customers who shop in multiple center outlets. One of the best shopping center points programs I have seen is at Gatwick Airport in London. Their Bonus Points program allows customers to earn points at Gatwick Airport when they park their car, make a purchase at most airport shops, buy food or drink at the airport's restaurants or bars, rent a car at the airport, or even exchange currency at any of the airport's bureaux de change. The accumulated points can be exchanged for frequent-flyer miles in any of the participating airline programs operated at Gatwick, any of the premium quality items available from a Bonus Points Privileges brochure, or vouchers redeemable at any of Gatwick's participating retail outlets. For travelers regularly flying through Gatwick, this program is an enticement to shop here, rather than in a shopping center nearer home.

Morgan's ESP Program

Two food retailers with highly successful partners and points programs are Morgan's Tuckerbag in Melbourne, Australia, and Superquinn in Dublin, Ireland.

Morgan's, with seven stores in five Melbourne suburbs, has developed a partnership program with over eighty of the area's businesses. Morgan's, the initiator of the program, invites one enterprise in each business category in the area where they operate to join the program on a renewable, six-month basis. According to Roger Morgan, CEO, the desire is to build a well-bonded, aggressive coalition of small business operators in the marketplace, promoting their ESP (Extra Shopping Power) card on a one-to-one basis. All businesses who join must make ESP a key element in promoting their business. Each program partner carries application forms, has ESP signage in his store and features ESP in his advertising.

Because this partnership program comprises smaller retailers covering such diverse areas of trade as shoes, sportswear, ceramics, furniture, curtains, insurance, a drugstore, a department store, hairdressers, and a jewelry chain, the program must be kept simple. The partners purchase sheets of stamps of ESP points. These stamps are issued to customers who affix them to a small card. As the cards are filled, they can be turned into "live" points at any of the Morgan's food outlets. Live points, in turn, can be redeemed for any of the large selection of attractive items in the gift showcases at the front of each of Morgan's stores or for gift certificates redeemable at any ESP partners' stores.

The program is an excellent example of how an umbrella of strength can be raised for independent operators without a loss of independence. And it greatly enhances the value of the card by providing ESP members the opportunity to accumulate points at a much faster rate than if they shopped at just one company's stores. It's a win-win situation for retailers and customers alike.

Superquinn and SuperClub

On the opposite side of the world from Morgan's is Ireland's Superquinn, the originating spark behind SuperClub. This is a group of retailers and service providers with the common objective of mutually enhancing one another's businesses. Current members include Superquinn, a sixteen-unit supermarket chain; Texaco, covering all of its gas outlets throughout Ireland; Atlantic Homecare, a chain of Do-It-Yourself super stores; the UCI Cinemas chain; McMahon+Nagel, one of Ireland's oldest and most respected window makers; the Irish Ferries; Coyle Hamilton, Ireland's leading insurance brokers; the National Irish Bank (which provides 20,000 SuperClub points when you take out a home loan from the bank!); a TV and home entertainment company, Cablelink; and two non-competing hotel groups, Great Southern Hotels and the Doyle Hotel Group. It also includes a car rental company, a coal company, a kitchen/bathroom/floor tile company, a travel agency, an auto dealership, and a women's apparel chain.

What diversity! But diversity with a common purpose—to allow customers to build points quickly to redeem the items in an attractive, 64-page gift catalog issued twice a year. Catalog items range from travel offers to cameras, from appliances to jewelry, from telephones to toys, and from wine to do-it-yourself items. Beside each item are a catalog number and the number of points required to acquire the product.

Readership of the catalog extends throughout Ireland, even though the base food retailer, Superquinn, is located only in the Dublin area. About 600,000 copies of the catalog are produced twice a year in a country with 1.1 million households, reflecting its widespread popularity.

A SuperClub member shopping at Superquinn receives points based upon her total purchases and additional points on hundreds of identified items around the store. When presenting her SuperClub card at the time of her transaction, a customer automatically has points added to her accumulated balance.

In like manner, a SuperClub member presenting her card to any of the other alliance members receives SuperClub points based upon the offering of the respective members. In most cases, the points are recorded electronically and are downloaded each evening to the SuperClub central computer. In other cases, the points are recorded on paper, which the member brings to a Superquinn store where a cashier scans the points into the member's account. For example, a SuperClub member going to a movie at any UCI cinema finds a number of points printed on her ticket which, on her next visit to Superquinn, can be added to her points total.

Members of the SuperClub alliance can structure their points according to the nature of their businesses. Single, double, or triple points may be issued on items, or on total spending, or a fixed number of points may be issued per transaction, regardless of its size. The range of options is very broad.

What is striking about both the Morgan's and the SuperClub programs is the diversity of their participants, which suggests the types of retailer and service organizations that can be part of your alliance are unlimited. Everyone, both customer and business, big or small, appears to come out ahead with a partners program.

Areas for concern

While benefits of a partners program are immense, two areas cause concern. First, the lack of a sophisticated computer interface to record points automatically wherever one shops is a problem. Both Morgan's and SuperClub overcame this difficulty through paper means. Second, ensuring that all the business participants keep the program at the center of their marketing strategy is necessary. It can be very tempting for a business to think it can get a free ride by sitting back and letting the other members give strong points incentives. This, of course, is short-sighted and is overcome by spelling out minimum participation requirements followed up with mystery shoppers validating that these requirements are being met.

5) Prizes

One primary goal of every retailer is to retain his existing customers—to get them to return on a regular basis. Sweepstakes, with their wide array of prizes, have been introduced to do just that.

Retailers with card programs have found that introducing a sweepstakes for their customers is relatively easy. Typically, computers provide an entry each time the cardholder uses her card. Non-cardholders who wish to participate have to take an extra step of filling out a paper entry form. Assuming attractive prizes and given the automatic entry feature, a sweepstakes program offers a retailer's cardholders another reason to drive past competitors to their store. It is one more competitive point of difference.

The million dollar sweepstakes

It certainly was a major point of difference for my mother-in-law between February and November, 1994, when one of her nearby food retailers, Big Y, ran a sweepstakes featuring a grand prize of $1 million—with significant other grand prizes, plus numerous weekly prizes of $1000 in cash, $50 gift certificates for groceries, and State lottery tickets. The possibility of winning $50,000 a year for the next twenty years was a deciding factor in where she shopped—as it was for many customers in western Massachusetts.

Not only did Big Y stand out with the magnitude of its grand prize, but the company also made it fun. A cardholder, for example, did not know whether she had won one of the fifteen $1,000 weekly cash prizes until her card was swiped the following week on her shopping visit. If the card carried a winning number, a red light started flashing from the ceiling and alarm bells sounded in the store! Everyone in the store stopped to see who the lucky winner was. (Who said that retailing has to be dull and boring?)

The million points sweepstakes

The grand prize does not have to be in cash to be attractive. Several years ago, Superquinn, in leveraging its point of difference, had a sweepstakes with the grand prize of one million SuperClub points. The winner could probably have taken one item of everything in the catalog and still have had points to spare!

Sweepstakes are becoming common

Sweepstakes are becoming common among food retailers. The interest in them has been so great that some of the database software providers, such as Darien, Connecticut-based RMS, have added a special sweepstakes package to their standard retail database offering.

Sweepstakes appear across the country, from the West to the East Coast. Vons, a major food retailer in southern California, regularly has sweepstakes offering travel-related prizes, ranging from vacations in Hawaii to Breakfast at Brennan's in New Orleans. It's a nice side benefit of food shopping!

On the other side of the country, Virginia-based Ukrop's rewards customers not just for shopping with them, but also for buying certain manufacturers' products. For example, Kraft may provide Ukrop's with some attractive prizes for the monthly sweepstakes. A Ukrop's Valued Customer cardholder receives one entry each time she shops at Ukrop's, and in addition, she receives one entry for each Kraft item she purchases during the sweepstakes period. To assist a customer in maximizing her chances of winning, the Kraft items are identified around the store with a colored bib-tag.

Interesting variations

One unique sweepstakes incorporating thresholds occurred during the recent 37th birthday anniversary celebrations of Foodtown Supermarkets in New Zealand. Only Foodtown cardholders were eligible (which is permitted by law in New Zealand). During the two weeks of birthday festivities, each cardholder received one entry for every $37 in each transaction. For example, a cardholder received one entry if her transaction was at least $37. She received two entries if her transaction was at least $74 and three entries if her transaction was at least $111. This promotion obviously favored the regular, bigger spending customer.

The emphasis of all of these sweepstakes is, as one retailer advertised, "Your card is your ticket!" Simply presenting the card automatically entered the customer into a sweepstakes. This is yet another layer of benefits for the card.

PetCare, an Aurora, Illinois-based pet superstore chain, has made a sweepstakes program its major point of difference. Customers are invited to apply for a *PetCare Happy Tails* card entitling them to one entry in the sweepstakes each time they shop and present their card. Prizes are store-based and each store draws ten winners weekly. Each store's grand prize is the winner's choice of a 11-20 lb. bag of dog food, a 6-10 lb. bag of cat food or $15 off any supply purchase. The two second prize winners can select from a 5-10 lb. bag of dog food, a 3-5 pound bag of cat food, or $7.50 off any supply purchase. And the seven third prize winners each week can select from a 2 lb. carton of dog treats, a 7 lb. container of cat litter, or $3.50 off any supply purchase.

This very creative, relatively low-cost card program appears to trigger a high card usage. The store does not offer any special prices for card members, just the opportunity to win a prize. It seems attractive to the customer, as the chance of winning a prize seems reasonable, given that they are store-based and drawn weekly. And the company benefits by being able to identify who their customers are, how often they shop, and how much they spend.

Areas of concern

Five areas of concern with sweepstakes should not be ignored:

1. Every state has certain laws and requirements regarding sweepstakes. Therefore, before launching a

sweepstakes, it is imperative that your proposed program is approved by a legal firm.

2. In some parts of the country, a strong antagonism towards lotteries and sweepstakes exists. If you think that a significant number of customers would object to a sweepstakes program, you may elect not to pursue it.

3. Interest in sweepstakes among customers appears to increase in proportion to the attractiveness of the prizes, as well as to the customers' perception of their chance of winning. It's a matter of behavior being influenced by the *chance* of a potential reward! This suggests that sweepstakes are more likely to be successful when run by larger companies because the magnitude of the prize, although not necessarily the chances of winning, appears so much greater.

4. If prizes are extremely attractive, your average transaction size may fall as customers spread their shopping over an increased number of visits to try to increase their odds of winning. This, of course, can be overcome by limiting the number of entries to each customer's first transaction on any day, or by awarding a number of the prizes based on a multiple of the winning transaction; for example, prizes which are one hundred times the amount of the winning purchase. In this case, the customer is rewarded for aggregating her purchases rather than breaking them into smaller orders.

5. Where the grand prizes are significant, a retailer may not want one of its employees to win one of the grand prizes, or any prize, because of the possible negative public perception. On the other hand, employees argue that they are customers and, as such, should be entitled to win like any other customer. Retailers have handled this issue in various ways. One retailer

excludes employees from winning any of the grand prizes, but they are eligible to win any of the lesser prizes. Another retailer excludes employees completely, arguing that the cash discounts they receive as employees put them in a separate category from regular customers and, therefore, they are not entitled to participate in the sweepstakes. Yet another progressive retailer, Platteville, Wisconsin-based Dick's, runs a sweepstakes just for employees. At the end of each quarter, all employees are entered into the sweepstakes which entitles the winners to one week's average wages for the quarter. Each employee receives one entry for each week in the quarter in which he or she spends at least $25 on the card.

6) Pro Bono

Retailers are constantly being approached for donations to support local charities, schools, and other worthy causes, resulting in cash donations, donations in kind, tapes-for-schools programs, fund raisers in the parking lot, and other forms of assistance.

Now, many card-based retailers are changing the nature of their donations programs for these good causes (*pro bono* means "for good") and are allocating their donations in proportion to what the supporters of these causes contribute to the company's sales. Today, retailers who can readily identify customer purchases are approaching this very sensitive subject in many ways, including:

• *Annual Giving.* One quarter each year, cardholders are invited to nominate the charity of their choice to which this food retailer will contribute 2% of their spending. At the end of the period, a list of donors, together with a check for the appropriate total, is sent to each of the nominated charities.

• *Computers for Schools.* A similar program run over a six- month period, but with the proceeds going to the customers' school of choice, rather than the charity of choice, was offered by another retailer. A variation of this was described earlier: Big Y's points-for-schools program, with points earned when cardholders purchased certain items that were identified around the store as points-for-schools products.

• *Specific Cause Donations.* Several years ago, one large retailer sponsored a campaign for children's cancer research. For every cardholder-identified item purchased, the company donated $0.03. A variation of this program, $0.05 per identified item, was seen a year later, with the proceeds going to the Salvation Army.

• *Community Groups.* Donations, in the form of gift certificates available to any community group, are yet another approach. In this case, the retailer offers the program for any two-month, pre-arranged period. The requirements are that the group must be a non-profit community interest or a sporting or religious group operating in the area. Two percent of the total purchases of the members of the group are returned to the group in the form of gift vouchers that may be redeemed in the retailer's stores. The retailer has one other qualifying stipulation—for every five existing cardholders put forward as members, the group must enroll one additional new member as a cardholder. Thus, if the group comprises 40 members, they must enroll eight new cardholders.

• *Church program.* During the first nine months each year, one retailer invites cardholders to nominate the church of their choice to which 1% of their total spending during the nine-month period is given. The program carries an interesting qualification—a cardholder must spend at least $250 during the nine-month period for her spending to be eligible for the donation. As you would expect, there has been an extremely positive response to this program, and it has been warmly encouraged by the preachers and church leaders.

• *Local fund-raiser.* A children's football league approached its local food retailer for a donation. The retailer wanted to help, but also wanted to test his newly installed card program at the same time. So he offered the league an amount equal to 5% off all private label sales during a specified four-week period. The retailer ran ads in the local paper and arranged signs and handbills, while the league members encouraged their friends and families to buy this retailer's private label products. Besides the children's football league receiving a handsome check, the retailer experienced a double-digit increase in private label sales, increased card usage, and a spike in new member sign-ups. In addition, the private label sales were at a higher level after the promotion than before. It's great to offer a program where everyone gains.

Words of caution

However, some words of caution are necessary regarding *pro bono* programs:

• Such programs on their own are seldom a critical differentiator in the eyes of customers in deciding long-term shopping loyalty. Therefore, be careful how much you allocate to such programs. Having to raise prices to subsidize a charitable program is unlikely to be a good business decision. Getting the right balance is very important.

• To reward your better customers more, introduce one or more thresholds for donation levels. For example, over a three-month period, it may be more prudent to give 1% of a cardholder's spending between $100 and $200, plus 2% between $200 and $300, plus 3% for all spending above $300.

• Avoid being locked into a *pro bono* program (or any other program) on a permanent basis. Plan breaks between such programs rather than having them run continuously throughout the year. A time break allows you to change the nature of the program or, when appropriate, withdraw it completely.

7) Privileges

All of us hunger for recognition. Privileges, receiving something exclusive because of our intrinsic worth, address this hunger and are greatly appreciated.

Over the past forty years, retailers with no systematic way of identifying their best customers were unable to express this appreciation. But now they can using information gained from card-based programs.

The widespread practice of offering privileges

Privileges for customers are not new in those business sectors which have had customer information for a long time. For example, when you stay at any of the Disney Resort hotels in Orlando, Florida, you are entitled to enter the Disney parks one hour earlier than everyone else. Not all of the exhibits are open, but the most popular ones are, which makes this a very powerful privilege—especially if you have your children with you! All you do is show your hotel pass at the entrance. The pass also entitles you to free parking at any of the Disney parks.

Occasionally, the CEO of Helzberg Diamonds, a highly successful Kansas City-based jewelry chain, sends his best customers an "Honorary Employee Discount Card." Employees receive a 25% discount at the chain year-round, and this special benefit is passed on to the honorary members for just one week. Customers love being singled out and show their appreciation, in turn, by using the card!

Harris Gordon, a frequent conference speaker on customer loyalty has, on several occasions, described how the most frequently sought-after privilege by the best customers at Neiman-Marcus is lunch with the store manager for the customer and two friends, followed by a private fashion show!

According to a story in the *Wall Street Journal* several years ago, Caesar's Palace penthouse in Las Vegas is available only to those who have at least a $1 million line of credit for gambling at the hotel. No exceptions are made to this rule. Not even wealthy film stars can buy their way into that penthouse. It is reserved only for those who have that impressive line of credit. The element of privilege and exclusivity touches even the wealthiest among us!

Marks and Spencer, one of the world's great retailers, has been very pleased with the strong response from their better customers who are invited to a special evening of shopping in their stores prior to Christmas. No special prices are offered. But the sense of exclusivity and privilege brings these special customers out in large numbers.

Green Hills Farms, with just one supermarket, was likewise overwhelmed with the reaction from its *best customers* when it closed its store early one evening after Thanksgiving last year and had a special appreciation evening. Customers were advised that the dress code was coat and tie. Employees, in formal wear, spent the evening mingling with them and serving food they prepared in the store. It was a showcase of their catering and unique foods capabilities. The cash registers were closed. Customers loved it so much that for many months afterwards they kept asking CEO Gary Hawkins whether this special evening would become an annual event.

The managing director and the marketing director of a leading department store chain each invite ten top customers every week into their board room for special appreciation luncheons. Management believes that getting to know twenty of their top customers each week in a setting like this strengthens customer bonds.

Privileges do not have to be grandiose to be appreciated. Something simple and sincere can work very effectively. Marv Imus, president of the Paw Paw Shopping Center, Paw Paw, Michigan, a single store operator, says he receives many sincere words of thanks from customers in response to his sending them, prior to their birthdays, a gift certificate inviting them to receive a free decorated birthday cake. The customer can call 24 hours in advance to indicate what wording she wants on the cake. What is so fascinating is that not only do customers appreciate this privilege but also the store benefits—total cake sales increased ten-fold in the first year of the program!

Surprise privileges

Surprise privileges seem to work particularly well when there is a reason for the surprise. These might include a special milestone, such as the customer's anniversary as a cardholder or when she reaches a certain spending threshold. Thoughtful thanks expressed in the form of a small floral arrangement on Valentine's Day, a free Thanksgiving turkey, a free Easter ham, a nice umbrella with the company logo on it, or even a simple but unique corkscrew for heavy wine buyers are other examples.

During the first November after the launch of his card program, one food retailer was so surprised to discover how much his very best customers were spending that he sent a note asking them to stop by their regular store to pick up a special Christmas gift—which they discovered, to their delight, was a bottle of Dom Pérignon champagne! Other very good customers received a special, but less expensive, bottle of champagne.

For those companies who offer cooking classes on a regular basis, one privilege might be to reserve several of the sessions each year just for the best customers.

The mailing of your company newsletter to the top 40-50% of your active customer base is also a form of privilege. So, too, is sending a colorful postcard to customers, letting them know that fresh strawberries (or fresh peaches, or...), with no mention of price, will be available the following week. On the postcard is your favorite recipe using this fruit.

Similarly, a gift certificate can be sent to your better customers, either by category or overall spending, inviting them to try a new product that has just been released. One retailer, in conjunction with a major manufacturer, mailed its top customers a free, full-size sample of a new product the manufacturer was launching. As the retailer quietly suggested, this was yet another privilege for loyal customers.

Privileges via the database
The opportunity to reward a retailer's best customers has not gone unnoticed outside retailing. Recently, the representative of a major airline approached one food retailer who had a high profile customer-card program. The airline was projecting surplus seating capacity, but did not want to start a competitive price war and discount its regular fares on the open market. Instead, they offered to sell part or all of that capacity on a private basis to the retailer via its card program. The retailer was

to send a letter to cardholders, advising them of this special private offer, inviting them to indicate whether they wished to participate. Each participant's spending would be tracked over the following twelve weeks, and in proportion to the amount spent, she would receive a significant discount off any regular airfare on this airline during the following twelve months.

An appropriation of American Express' tag line sums it up best: "Membership has its privileges!"

Caution is counseled

Privileges are a powerful differentiator. Therefore, prudence dictates that privileges are offered in a judicious and not a capricious manner. Most customers have a sense of fairness and will accept that some customers receive privileges for achievements such as reaching a certain spending level or being a long-time shopper. They are likely to become upset if they learn that privileges are being rewarded on an arbitrary basis or that certain customers are ineligible even if they meet the privilege criteria.

8) Personalization

The technological revolution is not just a matter of enabling customer data collection—it has also ushered in new point-of-sale systems with very open architecture which, among many other attractive features, provide customer information at the time of each transaction.

When a customer's card is scanned by the cashier at Lees Supermarket, in Westport, Massachusetts, for example, a greeting appears on the customer's screen: "Welcome to Lees, Mrs. Jones." The screen then shows, in large print, all of the items being scanned by the cashier.

At the same time, on the cashier's screen, in addition to what is being scanned, is the customer's name, and any other customer information that the Lees' father-and-son team think would add to the interaction of the cashier with the customer. For example, how long has the customer been a cardholder at Lees? Is she one of the store's best customers? How much over her order may a customer write a check without seeking management approval? *Such information can be personalized down to each individual customer.* The card is the key—not just for the special prices a customer receives, but also for the individualized personal attention she now receives as she checks out of the store.

Superquinn, which has a carryout service, has taken this one step further. Carhops are instructed to note the customer's name on the cashier's screen and after placing the customer's goods in her car, to use her name appropriately, such as "Thank you, Mrs. O'Malley, for shopping with us today!"

Personalization of the customer relationship is likely to become a great differentiator in the marketplace. It seems ironic that cold, impersonal technology is being used to warm the retailer's relationship with his customers. The same technology that triggers the response in hotels when calling the operator or room service, "Good evening, Mr. Woolf. How may I help you?" is now being applied to retailing. The Automatic Number Identification (ANI) concept in hotels, which enables the operator to know your name because of the room number you call from, is allowing retailing employees to know each customer's name because of the card that she presents.

One variation of this personalization of the customer relationship is currently being refined by Mark Dodge,

CEO of Easy Access, New London, Wisconsin. After developing kiosks for a Wisconsin food retailer, Mark has now established his own kiosk company. Recently he was telling me that it is quite simple to program the store manager's beeper to activate when any particular customer, or group of customers, swipe their card at the kiosk as they walk in the store. This means that a store manager will now be able to greet, on the shop floor, preselected customers with corner-grocer friendliness in this age of impersonal, huge, high-tech stores.

How well do we know our customers?

Many store managers believe they know the faces, if not the names, of their best customers. When Albert Lees, Jr., the Chairman of Lees Supermarket, introduced a frequent-shopper card program a few years ago, in response to a challenge that he wouldn't know them all, he wrote down the names of his top ten customers. "Of course I know them, " he exclaimed, "I've been running this store for forty years!"

Later, to his chagrin, he discovered that he knew only four of his top ten customers. He couldn't put a face to the names of the other six! He didn't even know his top customer who was spending over $10,000 a year in his store! He did know those who complained a lot but, as he discovered, didn't spend very much.

Now that we have the technology, why shouldn't a store management team know at least the faces, if not the names, of the top 1% of their customers who provide up to 10% of their store's sales?

Getting to know you

How can we get to know our customers better? One large specialty retailer has a team of over forty people who spend all of their time just calling customers! Based upon their knowledge of customer activity, they are calling them, thanking them for being a good customer, finding out what they thought of their last visit, seeking ideas for new products to be stocked in the stores, etc. This company is showing a proactive "We Care" personalization. Is money spent on such personalized research and caring better spent than on newspaper ads? Without a doubt!

Various food retailers are moving down the same path. Each week, one card-based retailer sends the manager of each store the names and phone numbers of that store's top five customers in the previous week. The manager, or a very personable member of the store team, calls and spends as much as twenty minutes discussing the store with each one! The customer is usually very surprised, but very appreciative, that she received a call from her supermarket asking how she enjoyed her last visit, whether she found everything she wanted, and whether she had any suggestions for improving her shopping experience. The caller makes notes on a one-page summary sheet, and all calls are later discussed by the store management team. This contact also provides an opportunity for the manager to arrange to meet the customer when she is next in the store.

The names of the contacted customers are tagged in the database, so that they cannot be called again during the following thirty weeks. Therefore, over a thirty-week period, the store is in direct contact with, and learns more about, its top 150 customers. The best customers are transformed from statistical transactions at the checkouts to flesh and blood reality. This is yet another example of how information is transforming the face of retailing, and how traditional retailers are becoming increasingly vulnerable to those armed with customer information.

Personalization can also help your *defection prevention program.* Several times a month, one store manager reviews the list of the top 10% of his customers, and identifies those who have not shopped with him during the latest 6-8 weeks. He then picks up the phone, calls them and in a very nice way finds out why they have not recently been in his store.

The ability to identify changes in customers' shopping behavior on an exceptional basis and to communicate with them in this way, makes me believe that the store manager of the future will be just as responsible for filling his aisles with customers as filling his shelves with products!

Pitfalls to avoid

Of course, some pitfalls should be avoided in this move towards customer personalization. The first is indicating to the customer that you know too much about them. For example, if you find customers who have stopped shopping in your meat department and you wish to find out why, calling and asking them "Why have you stopped shopping in our meat department?" may well trigger the end of their relationship with you because they feel that their privacy has been invaded. However, a telephone call thanking the customer for her business and asking her for an assessment of each department in your store would achieve the same objective in an oblique, but pleasant, manner. Customers are aware that they have left an enormous trail of activity in the marketplace, ranging from credit cards to checks to frequent-shopper cards. They just don't like being reminded about it!

A second pitfall to avoid is becoming overly friendly or over-communicative with your customers, thereby creating what's called the *hedgehog effect*. We can get too close to the customer so that, like hedgehogs, we start to prickle and hurt each other. One colleague reminded me of this recently. She had received three calls from a large home improvement chain within a two-week period. The calls were from different departments. They were either following up on an area of concern or asking whether she enjoyed her shopping experience. The third call started to annoy her. She didn't want so many calls from one retailer. "Why can't they coordinate their calls?" she complained. This suggests that, as companies make personalization an integral element of their strategy, they will need to introduce a central coordinating telephone log to avoid the hedgehog effect.

9) Participation

Customer participation in your business can range from the simple to the sophisticated—from the sign in the produce department in Lees Supermarket which reads, "If you find anything in the produce department that is not up to your standards, please dump it in this bin," to Dallas, Texas-based Southwest Airlines, which involves its best customers in the employee selection process. Both involve the customer in improving operations. Both make the statement that they care about how their customers feel about their company.

Customers do have opinions about our stores. They do wonder why we retailers do dumb things at times. And they do want an easy way to express their opinions to help us do better. Part of the reason for this is they have already invested their time in a relationship with us and are prepared to invest even more. Allowing them to do just that in any area of our business, from product selection to store design, not only enriches our understanding of our customers' desires, but also strengthens the customer bond with our business.

The breakthrough

For retailers with customer databases, the breakthrough that has occurred in recent years is that we can now encourage customer participation on a rational basis. We can, for example, invite our customers to participate in our store advisory boards based upon their shopping behavior with us, rather than simply having those who volunteer. Our selection process can be based on, say, how often a customer has shopped with us in the last twelve months or on how much she has spent. With this information, we can now weigh their input based upon their shopping activity.

In like manner, customer surveys, both written and by telephone, can be directed to customers with specific activity profiles.

Customer participation can take many forms. One retailer sends a small questionnaire, along with a gift certificate, to his first-time customers. They are asked to evaluate the front-end service on their next store visit. In this way, the company is constantly receiving a fresh viewpoint of this critical service area from new customers who obviously have a valuable external perspective. This feedback is critically important when you consider that food retailers lose over 50% of new customers within twelve months! Knowing how customers view just one aspect of your service will help address this serious erosion problem.

You can start seeking customer participation in your merchandise offering by sending a questionnaire to the top 20% of your customers, asking them what items they cannot find in your stores and must purchase elsewhere. When such products later appear on the shelves, these top customers recognize that they have participated in the decision-making process and, as a result, their affinity with you is strengthened. You have just moved up another step on the differentiation ladder in that customer's mind.

Recently, one retailer was evaluating a new private-label salsa. He had five different flavors proposed to him. Which one should he choose? He didn't. Instead, he went to his database, identified the eight largest purchasers of salsa and invited them in for a taste testing. He let them decide which of the flavors should carry the company's elite private label. After all, they were the ones who were going to buy the largest quantities of the salsa!

A similar review can be made of your wine offering. Why not have a special wine and cheese evening for your top wine customers and discover which wines they like but have to buy elsewhere. This information will never appear on your store's scan data. In addition, the mere invitation to participate in this review enhances the bond between you and your customer.

Another participation possibility is to invite customers to join a customer privacy panel, set up to ensure that customer data is handled in a sensitive, secure manner.

Customers can be invited to send in their favorite recipe, to be included in a recipe book compiled and sold by your company with the proceeds going to a different charity each year.

Morgan's Tuckerbag has a special box placed next to its gift showcase for customers' suggestions regarding showcase additions. One charming older lady indicated she needed a manual egg beater. One was quickly added!

200,000 quality control experts

My favorite example of participation is seen at Superquinn. Earlier, I described how the company introduced a program which gave 100 point SuperClub certificates to customers who found specific problems while shopping—such as refrigeration temperature checks not done on time or having to wait more than a certain time in a checkout line. After eighteen months with this program, Feargal Quinn and his team took the ultimate step in customer participation: they offered any customer a 100 point SuperClub certificate for *anything* the customers believed was wrong in the store! The outcome is that Superquinn, one of the world's leading-edge companies in customer relations, has now added close to 200,000 quality control experts each week who evaluate their stores and participate in making Superquinn a better place to shop!

10) Presto

One of the many by-products of the myriad technological developments is that the customer's *bar of expectations* is constantly being raised. Visit any retailer today who doesn't have scanning, and you think they are either old-fashioned or going out of business. Shop in a store with a sophisticated frequent-shopper card program where prices are automatically discounted for you, points are automatically accumulated, and the up-to-the-minute balance of your accumulated points is printed on the bottom of your register tape. Then visit a competing retailer who is still bogged down with a paper or cardboard card which the cashier has to clip to indicate you have shopped there. You feel like you have gone from a first world retailer to a third world store.

The emphasis on promptness or speed—the Presto factor—and on having all relevant information updated at the end of each and every transaction is the tenth measure of differentiation on our new battlefield.

Retailers are beginning to echo McDonald's great slogan, "We do it all for you"—but instantaneously! After all, if a retailer can swipe a customer's credit card and establish the customer's credit worthiness at that very moment, regardless of where or how often the customer has shopped earlier that day, then, so too, should retailers seek the same level of speed with their frequent-shopper cards.

No retailer to my knowledge has yet developed the Presto factor to an art form. However, a number are actively moving in this direction, as they understand that time-based marketing is another important tool in their marketing toolbag.

Focusing on the Presto factor is not the exclusive domain of large retailers. Consider Rolf Holmberg's two Flygfyren supermarkets near Stockholm, Sweden. His Gold Club cardholders accumulate points based upon their total purchases, as well as their purchase of selected merchandise around the store. Twice a year, in February and August, when a Gold Card customer presents her card, the cashier asks, "Would you like the discount you have earned on the purchases you made in the past six months taken off this transaction?"

His computer system not only tracks all activity on each customer's card over each six-month period, but calculates the proportional rewards due on the points as well. And this appears automatically on the cashier's screen on the first visit the customer makes to the store after the close of the six-month period! It is a completely paperless, instantaneous process. The customer has no coupons to clip or vouchers to carry. Everything is done electronically. Rolf Holmberg has created a new level of expectation for all of his customers when they shop elsewhere.

Big Y Supermarkets have raised the competitive bar in their market area for redeeming triple coupons. The customer no longer has to waste time sorting her coupons to find the three with the highest value, as is necessary at various competitors; Big Y's point-of-sale equipment automatically gives cardholders triple credit for the three highest value coupons presented!

Another retailer in the Northeast, who regularly offers continuity programs, has developed software so that customers receive any entitlement on their continuity program up to, and including, the transaction they are in the midst of processing. Being an on-line, real-time retailer adds yet another arrow to the quiver of differentiators.

Ours is an instant-pudding society. We want things now! Progressive retailers will always find ways to match, and exceed, their customers' expectations.

Bundle marketing

As this chapter suggests, Pandora's technology box has been opened, releasing ten major marketing points of difference. All of them were, theoretically, available to retailers in yesterday's era of mass marketing, but the simplicity, speed and sophistication of today's computers make it easy to use these ten new tools.

The common denominator of the *ten P's* is information, allowing us to rewrite the rules of retailing. There is no going back. We can only embrace the future.

The challenge confronting us is how to win in this information-rich, competitive environment. How can we take advantage of the imperfect information in the marketplace? How should we balance the *ten P's* in our offer-bundle? How can we leverage, in our customer's eyes, our deliberately chosen key point of difference? How can we keep layering value around our card? How can we keep changing the battlefield to best suit our evolving strengths?

Part IV: Measurements

This section introduces you to the new measurements available with customer information and shows how this information will impact your company's organization structure.

Chapter 8 walks you through a series of detailed tables that will become your new retail compass.

Chapter 9 describes how we will reorganize our businesses around customers instead of products.

8

Your new retail compass

"The road to success is paved with good information." This old expression has never rung so true. The amount of information now becoming available is overwhelming. We need a compass to guide us to what is crucial in understanding and managing our businesses better, using customer data. The aim of this chapter is to provide such guidelines.

Companies such as Darien, Connecticut-based RMS (203-656-3411) and Dallas, Texas-based S2 Systems Inc. (800-527-4131) offer excellent software packages with the standard reports a retailer needs to run a successful differentiated marketing program.

Alternatively, if you prefer to move into customer specific marketing with the assistance of a service bureau, as many do, there's Manasquan, New Jersey-based DCI (908-449-2525). Founded in 1971 by Paul W. Corliss, a pioneer in card-based marketing, DCI offers *Datamagic*, a PC-based reporting and target marketing support system. They provide other helpful services as well, including targeted direct mail, and analysis and reporting of customer information.

Another full-service company that supports a lot of card-based marketing programs is Moore BCS (203-378-1518). Talking to each of these companies, and others, will provide a good range of options as you think through what's best for your circumstances. And all of these companies are constantly upgrading their reporting capabilities in response to their clients' ever-escalating needs. In addition, other database providers, sensing the huge opportunity here, are rushing to develop new database packages for this exploding market.

If you wish to develop your own standard reports from your database, Tables 8-1 through 8-6 are what I consider the basic reports for differentiated marketers. These reports, or variations of them, are standard in any package from any leading retail-oriented software house or service bureau.

Each table is described in some depth. If you are not interested in such a detailed discussion at this time, *please turn to page 125* to the section headed *Beyond the six reports* where you can read of some interesting ways retailers are beginning to use customer information to improve their results.

Table 8-1: Cardholders' Performance Report

Table 8-1 measures the percentage of transactions and sales captured on your card and shows how each store is performing against the average of the district, region or company during the latest four and twelve weeks.

In Table 8-1, each store is compared to the average results of the nineteen-store district to allow us to identify which stores are doing poorly or well, and to see the changes in these trends.

To understand the report, let's refer to Redville. The cardholders of this store accounted for 56.9% of transactions and 89.3% of sales in the past four weeks. Their transaction performance was better than the twelve-week 55.5% result, which tells us that the store has been improving its data capture ability in recent weeks.

| Cardholders' Performance Report | XYZ Stores | | Table 8 - 1 |

Review Period: 4 & 12 weeks ending 31 Mar 1999

Performance Base for Averages is: **District** / Region / Company

Performance Base:	4 wks	12 wks
% Trans	56.8	55.1
% Sales	79.1	78.2
# Stores	19	19

West Zone Stores	Actual Store Performance				Variance from Avg. Performance				Performance Ranking			
	% Total Trans.		% Total Sales		% Total Trans.		% Total Sales		For % Trans.		For % Sales	
Store	4 wks	12 wks	4 wks	12 wks	4 wks	12 wks	4 wks	12 wks	4 wks	12 wks	4 wks	12 wks
Redville	56.9	55.5	89.3	87.6	0.1	0.4	10.2	9.4	7	9	2	2
Blueville	53.2	51.1	72.6	71.1	(3.6)	(4.0)	(6.5)	(7.1)	14	17	15	17
Pinkville	50.3	54.0	69.3	77.2	(6.5)	(1.1)	(9.8)	(1.0)	15	11	17	11
Grayville	56.0	51.4	78.5	76.9	(0.8)	(3.7)	(0.6)	(1.3)	9	16	10	12
Goldville	63.5	60.8	92.1	91.6	6.7	5.7	13.0	13.5	2	2	1	1
Greenville	54.3	57.2	74.3	77.3	(2.5)	2.1	(4.8)	(0.9)	11	7	13	10
Orangeville	47.4	42.1	64.2	59.4	(9.4)	(13.0)	(14.9)	(18.8)	19	19	19	19

The average performance of the nineteen stores in the district is seen in the box at the top right. Redville's cardholder transaction results were just ten basis points (0.10%) better than the district average of 56.8% for the past four weeks, but its percentage of sales on the card of 89.3% was 1020 basis points (10.20%) higher than the district average. This means that during the past four weeks, even though Redville was seventh of the nineteen stores for the percentage of total transactions recorded on the card, it ranked second for percentage of sales on the card.

The table also shows the variances from the average performance to identify how much better or worse each store is compared with the average and how this changes over time. Similarly, the performance ranking gives a quick visual check of changes in the relative performance for each store.

Table 8-2: The Bathtub Report

Once the majority of our transactions are on the card, even though new cardholder applications continue to come in every week, the percentage of transactions on the card does not keep rising rapidly because some customers stop shopping with us.

Based upon my research with food retailers, customers who don't shop for twelve consecutive weeks have about a 10% chance of returning. Therefore, to learn how many customers are active at any one time, as opposed to how many customers have been issued cards since our program began, Table 8-2, the Bathtub Report, was introduced.

The Bathtub Report permits us to identify:

• *How many new members sign up for the card each week.* We see that new customers per store averaged 180 in the week ended (W/E) January 7 this year (TY)

The Bathtub Report — Members Net Additions — XYZ Stores

Table 8 - 2

Averages Per Store

Inactive = not shopped during the past 12 weeks

	For W/E	New Members TY	New Members LY	- Inactive Members TY	- Inactive Members LY	+ Reactivated Members TY	+ Reactivated Members LY	= Net Chg. for Week TY	= Net Chg. for Week LY	= Active Members at End of Week TY	= Active Members at End of Week LY	This Year Better (Worse) Than Last Year (% change) New	Inact.	React.	Net	Tot.
1	7-Jan	180	160	(230)	(180)	20	10	(30)	(10)	9,970	7,990	12.5	(27.8)	100.0	(200.0)	24.8
2	14-Jan	130	145	(120)	(113)	15	24	25	56	9,995	8,046	(10.3)	(6.2)	(37.5)	(55.4)	24.2
3	21-Jan	156	121	(150)	(174)	0	12	6	(41)	10,001	8,005	28.9	13.8	(100.0)	NM	24.9
4	28-Jan	148	103	(150)	(100)	14	10	12	13	10,013	8,018	43.7	(50.0)	40.0	(7.7)	24.9
5	4-Feb	107	114	(140)	(200)	8	0	(25)	(86)	9,988	7,932	(6.1)	30.0	NM	70.9	25.9
6	11-Feb	132	131	(102)	(149)	0	8	30	(10)	10,018	7,922	0.8	31.5	(100.0)	NM	26.5
7	18-Feb	121	109	(141)	(101)	24	0	4	8	10,022	7,930	11.0	(39.6)	NM	(50.0)	26.4
8	25-Feb	100	94	(138)	(73)	10	9	(28)	30	9,994	7,960	6.4	(89.0)	11.1	NM	25.6
9	4-Mar	98	87	(91)	(76)	8	15	15	26	10,009	7,986	12.6	(19.7)	(46.7)	(42.3)	25.3
10	11-Mar	125	84	(141)	(98)	15	11	(1)	(3)	10,008	7,983	48.8	(43.9)	36.4	66.7	25.4
11	18-Mar	137	102	(116)	(81)	26	9	47	30	10,055	8,013	34.3	(43.2)	188.9	56.7	25.5
12	25-Mar	114	96	(149)	(132)	30	18	(5)	(18)	10,050	7,995	18.8	(12.9)	66.7	72.2	25.7
13	4 W/E									10,000	8,000					25.0
						Figures as at beginning of first week (above)										
14	28-Jan	614	529	(650)	(567)	49	56	13	18	10,013	8,018	16.1	(14.6)	(12.5)	(27.8)	24.9
15	25-Feb	460	448	(521)	(523)	42	17	(19)	(58)	9,994	7,960	2.7	0.4	147.1	67.2	25.6
16	25-Mar	474	369	(497)	(387)	79	53	56	35	10,050	7,995	28.5	(28.4)	49.1	60.0	25.7

compared with 160 per store in the same week last year (LY).

• *How many customers became inactive each week.* On January 7 this year 230 customers per store had not shopped with us at any time during the previous twelve weeks, compared to 180 in the same twelve-week period last year.

• *How many customers who previously went inactive have returned to shop with us.* In the week ending January 7, 20 such customers reactivated this year, compared to 10 per store last year.

After adding the 180 new members to the 20 reactivated members and subtracting the 230 customers who went inactive during the week of January 7, we had a net loss of 30 active customers. At the beginning of the year we had 10,000 active customers, which means that at the end of the first week, we had an average of 9,970 active customers per store. In other words, 9,970 cardholders (per store) shopped with us at least once in the twelve weeks ending January 7. This number is a *critical indicator* of future sales because it tells us the level of active customers from which our sales will be drawn. This level of active customers rises (and falls) weekly—thus the term *bathtub.*

The right-hand section of Table 8-2 records the year-to-year percentage changes of the various left-hand columns. These better (worse) percentage columns help us understand the changes in our customer behavior on a weekly basis. For example, we can measure how effectively our new customer addition programs are working this year compared to last year by looking at the percentage change in new members. It also acts as a customer satisfaction barometer in that it shows whether the number of customers going inactive is increasing or decreasing on a year-to-year basis.

Executives at one large food retailer study this report very carefully on a store-by-store basis at their monthly management meetings. They scrutinize their customer inflows and outflows, seeking to understand the changes in each store's sales performance.

Be aware that if you run the Bathtub Report for each individual store, the sum of customers who become inactive is usually greater than the number who become inactive on a company-wide basis. This is because a certain number of customers move from store to store. They may shop at one store for awhile, then switch to another. Therefore, if you wish to run such a report for each individual store, you will need to measure two types of customer defections: internal and external. The total of external defections should equal the numbers shown in the Bathtub Report. Internal defections need to be counted and assessed separately.

Table 8-3: The RFS Decile Report

After recording the percentages of transactions and sales on our card and learning how our customers are flowing into and out of our stores, the third basic measurement report is the RFS Decile Report, Table 8-3, which provides us with a profile of our customers. RFS stands for Recency, Frequency, and Sales, the three basic pillars of customer segmentation.

In this example, an average of 15,000 cardholders per store shopped at least once during the twelve-week review period. These customers are broken into ten equal groups, or deciles, based upon how much they have spent over the twelve-week review period.

The customers in the top decile (decile 10) spent an average of $69.06 per week, while those customers in the bottom decile (decile 1), spent an average of $1.08 per week over the twelve-week period. Customers in decile 10 shopped an average of 1.78 times per week and

RFS Decile Report — XYZ Stores

Review Period: 12 weeks ending 31 Mar 1999

Table 8 - 3

Results: (1) include new customers; (2) are averages per store

Sales Annualization Factor: 0.80

Dec-ile (#)	Custs. (#)	Trans. (#k)	Sales ($k)	Trans. (%)	Sales (%)	Cum.Trans. (%)	Cum Sales (%)	Recency Days since last visit	Frequency Visits Per Week	Avg. Trans.	Spending Per Week	Spending Per Year	ASPI ($)
10	1,500	32.0	1,243	29.8%	42.2%	29.8%	42.2%	1.8	1.78	$38.80	$69.06	$2,873	1.86
9	1,500	21.2	591	19.8%	20.1%	49.6%	62.3%	2.9	1.18	27.84	32.85	$1,367	1.75
8	1,500	14.9	370	13.9%	12.6%	63.5%	74.9%	3.9	0.83	24.75	20.54	$855	1.71
7	1,500	11.5	262	10.7%	8.9%	74.2%	83.8%	7.1	0.64	22.77	14.57	$606	1.68
6	1,500	8.8	185	8.2%	6.3%	82.4%	90.1%	10.1	0.49	21.00	10.29	$428	1.66
5	1,500	6.5	129	6.0%	4.4%	88.4%	94.5%	12.9	0.36	19.84	7.14	$297	1.64
4	1,500	4.3	76	4.0%	2.6%	92.5%	97.0%	16.3	0.24	17.54	4.21	$175	1.63
3	1,500	3.2	37	3.0%	1.3%	95.5%	98.3%	19.5	0.18	11.56	2.08	$87	1.61
2	1,500	2.7	31	2.5%	1.0%	98.0%	99.3%	23.7	0.15	11.30	1.70	$71	1.57
1	1,500	2.2	19	2.0%	0.7%	100.0%	100.0%	30.1	0.12	8.98	1.08	$45	1.40
Tot.	15,000	107.5	$2,943	100.0%	100.0%			12.8	0.60	$27.39	$16.35	$680	1.76
Avg. Per Wk.		9.0	$245										

spent an average of $38.80 per transaction over the twelve-week period (note: 1.78 x $38.80 = $69.06).

The Recency column shows that our average top customer was most recently in our stores 1.8 days before the end of the twelve-week period. In contrast, the average customer in our bottom decile last visited us 30.1 days before the end of the review period.

The extreme right-hand column shows that the average selling price of items (ASPI) sold to our best customers during the review period was $1.86, which was 33% greater than the $1.40 to the customers in our bottom decile.

To the left of the ASPI column is the annualized spending column. This shows us that our best customers, based upon the twelve-weeks results, are projected to spend $2,873 in the current year. This figure is calculated by multiplying the *spending per week* by 52 weeks by the *sales annualization factor* ($69.06 x 52 x 0.80 = $2,873). The sales annualization factor is inserted because it is not valid to extrapolate the last twelve weeks' results with a straight line projection to arrive at the 52-week sales projection. This is because in the following forty weeks customers go on vacation, stop shopping at the company, and so forth, and these variations must be included when projecting annual sales from a twelve-week base. Your company's annualization factor depends upon your customer retention rate and the season on which your projection is based.

On the left-hand side of Table 8-3 are the transactions and sales columns. They show the number of transactions and sales generated by each decile over the review period. The example shows that the top decile comprised 29.8% of all cardholder transactions and 42.2% of all cardholder sales. The next two columns are these percentages recorded on a cumulative basis.

117

The RFS Decile Report clearly illustrates how customers in the top decile record, like clockwork, better performances (in every column) than those in the next best decile, and this experience continues all the way down to the bottom decile. Because the relative performance of each decile is as predictable as clockwork, we call this *clockwork economics.*

The value of this report lies in providing management with an understanding of their customer dynamics. It also acts as an excellent scorecard of your marketing activities at different customer levels.

Table 8-4: The Quo Vadis Retention Report

The Quo Vadis Retention Report, Table 8-4, is a very powerful analytical report that tells us not just how many customers have stopped shopping with us, but also from what customer groups these defections have occurred. It also tells us, of the customers who stayed, what percentage increased and decreased their spending this year over last, and what percentage spent the same amount. Thus the report name, *Quo Vadis* (a Latin term meaning *whither goest*).

Table 8-4, the actual results for a very successful food retailer, shows that for every 1,000 customers in the twelve weeks ending September 4, 1993, only 706 customers came back in the same twelve-week period a year later; 294 did not. This is a defection rate of 29.4%—a lot of lost customers!

One of the first questions management should ask when hearing of this high defection rate is, "Which customers have we lost—our highest or lowest spenders?"

Reading the defection column from top to bottom, we see that the top 20% (top quintile) of customers had a *defection rate* of only 4%. This means that 4% of the best customers in this quarter last year did not shop with us

Quo Vadis Retention Report

XYZ Stores

Table 8 - 4

Review Periods:

12 weeks ending Sep 4, 1993

12 weeks ending Sep 3, 1994

		Customers LY
For every	1,000	
This year	706	Came back
External Defections =	294	
~ Retention Rate	70.6%	
~ Defection Rate	29.4%	

Spending Per Week

LY Threshold >	$31.87	$17.45	$6.44	$2.50	$0.01		
Quintiles	5	4	3	2	1	Defections	Totals
Gold = Best	Gold	Silver	Bronze	Copper	Tin		
5 Gold	74%	16%	4%	1%	1%	4%	100%
4 Silver	17%	45%	18%	6%	4%	10%	100%
3 Bronze	4%	20%	29%	16%	8%	24%	100%
2 Copper	1%	6%	16%	20%	13%	44%	100%
1 Tin	1%	2%	6%	12%	15%	64%	100%
Totals	97%	89%	73%	55%	41%	29%	100%

at all in the same quarter this year. Compare this with the 10% defection rate from the next quintile (the Silver quintile), the 24% defection rate from the Bronze (middle) quintile, 44% from the Copper quintile, and a horrifying (but normal!) defection rate of 64% from the lowest spending 20% of customers.

The results seen in Table 8-4 are common among food retailers today. Highest spending customers have the lowest defection rates. The lowest spending, the Copper and Tin customers, have the highest defection rates. This is ironic because it's to this bottom 40% with the highest defection rates that most retailers apply the majority of their advertising and markdown monies!

Another question usually asked when looking at this report is: "Has customer spending increased or decreased this year?" This can be answered quintile by quintile. For example, only 45% of the Silver (second best) quintile spent the same amount this year as last (between $17.45 and $31.87 per week). Fortunately, 17% of last year's Silver customers increased their weekly spending to above $31.87 this year, but 18% of last year's Silver customers dropped their spending to the Bronze (middle) level this year; 6% dropped their spending to only $2.50-$6.44 per week (the Copper level), and 4% dropped to the lowest spending Tin level.

Researching changes in customer behavior

The Quo Vadis Report also allows a retailer to identify and research changes in customer behavior. For example, the retailer could use a telephone or mail survey to learn why 6% of last year's Silver customers dropped their spending to the Copper (second bottom) level this year. Then, using that information, the retailer could develop an appropriate targeted offer just to them.

Similarly, because our top-tiered Gold customers are so valuable, research to determine why 4% of them have defected would be extremely valuable. What portion of this 4% was due to *involuntary* causes such as death, moving out of our market area, or a significant life style change; and how much was due to *voluntary* changes, such as switching to a competitor?

Other Quo Vadis report uses

Even though the Quo Vadis Report shows quarterly, year-to-year comparisons, some retailers also use this report to measure changes from one quarter to the next—to see short-term changes in behavior and to measure the slippage in each quintile's spending levels.

Yet another retailer uses the report to measure and identify customer losses when a competitor opens against them. He sets the initial review period as the twelve weeks prior to the competitor's opening and then monitors the customer erosion after the competitor starts trading. Appropriate customer recapture programs are then introduced for selected cells in the report.

Another use of the Quo Vadis Retention Report is to monitor changes in the spending patterns and defection rates of new customers. For example, if we take customers who first use their cards during the first quarter of the year and calculate their actual weekly spending, we can jump to the third quarter and profile them. We can learn such things as: how many of our new customers have defected; how many high spending new customers we lost; and, of those new customers still with us, how have they changed their spending levels.

The Quo Vadis Report can also be a valuable tool at the department level. One retailer, for example, is using this report to monitor changes in each of his departments on a quarter-to-quarter basis.

Such uses of this report gives us a flavor of the creativity that retailers with customer databases are applying to the new information now available.

By identifying customer movements between cells of the Quo Vadis Report, we can learn more about our customers' behavior, develop programs to build their business with us and then, in subsequent quarters, measure the effectiveness of our actions. What a great manifestation of customer specific marketing!

Table 8-5: The New Member Frequency Report

There is a false cry for new customers on the lips of most retailers. Many new customers enter our stores every week. The problem is most don't return. I have found that half of a food retailer's new customers typically defect within a year! Consider the results of one leading differentiated marketer: for every 100 customers who presented their card for the first time in the twelve weeks ending September, 1993, only 37 shopped in the same quarter in 1994, and only 33 shopped in the same quarter in 1995. This was a 63% year-to-year *new member defection rate* in the first year (1993-4), and a 10% year-to-year defection rate in the second year (1994-5). The two-year (1993-5) defection rate was 67%.

The New Member Frequency Report, Table 8-5, was designed to measure the return frequency of your new customers. This is the first step in addressing this serious loss problem.

Table 8-5, which records how often new members shop in their first twelve weeks, shows that of the 105 new cardholders per store who first used their card in the week ending January 7, 50.5% of them shopped only once! They came in, signed up for the card, used it once and never returned in the twelve-week period. And 19.0% shopped only two or three times in the same twelve-week period. And so on.

New Member Frequency Report — XYZ Stores

Table 8 - 5

How often do our new members visit us in their first 12 weeks?

No. of Stores in last week of Review Period: 15

Card first used in W/E	12 wks to W/E	New Mem. Per Store	Total Number of Visits in 12-week period by New Members (% of total)						
			1 VPW=.08	2-3 0.17-0.25	4-5 0.33-.42	6-8 0.50-.67	9-11 0.75-.92	12-17 1.00-1.42	18+ >1.50
7-Jan	25-Mar	105	50.5%	19.0%	22.9%	7.6%	0.0%	0.0%	0.0%
14-Jan	1-Apr	102	38.2	21.6	17.6	5.9	14.7	2.0	0.0
21-Jan	8-Apr	95	41.1	17.9	20.0	4.2	11.6	2.1	3.2
28-Jan	15-Apr	87	46.0	11.5	14.9	3.4	10.3	10.3	3.4
4-Feb	22-Apr	99	60.6	13.1	21.2	2.0	3.0	0.0	0.0
11-Feb	29-Apr	103	41.7	21.4	12.6	9.7	11.7	2.9	0.0
18-Feb	6-May	78	55.1	9.0	11.5	10.3	5.1	6.4	2.6
25-Feb	13-May	98	34.7	15.3	25.5	8.2	5.1	9.2	2.0
4-Mar	20-May	110	46.4	10.9	12.7	7.3	6.4	7.3	9.1
11-Mar	27-May	81	53.1	21.0	8.6	3.7	8.6	1.2	3.7
18-Mar	3-Jun	89	44.9	18.0	18.0	6.7	4.5	3.4	4.5
25-Mar	10-Jun	95	52.6	18.9	10.5	6.3	3.2	6.3	2.1
1-Apr	17-Jun	108	51.9	12.0	13.9	4.6	8.3	9.3	0.0
Average %		100.0%	47.3%	16.2%	16.3%	6.2%	7.1%	4.6%	2.3%
Avg. # Members		96	45	16	16	6	7	4	2

Cardholders Summary Report		XYZ Stores		Table 8-6	

Review Period: 4 weeks ended 31 Mar 1999

	Results Per Trading Week	This Year	Last Year	Better (Worse) #	Better (Worse) %
1	Cardholder Transactions as % Total Transactions	64.3%	56.8%	7.5%	13.2%
2	Cardholder Sales as % Total Sales	88.9%	82.5%	6.4%	7.8%
3	Latest 12-week Defection Rate (Last Year to This Year)	22.30%	29.54%	(7.2%)	24.5%
4	Latest 12-week Defection Rate (Last Qtr. to This Qtr.)	9.59%	11.65%	(2.1%)	17.7%
5	Cardholder Spending Per Visit (SPV)	$31.43	$28.00	$3.43	12.3%
6	Active Cardholders Visits Per Week (last 4 weeks)	0.92	0.88	0.04	4.5%
7	Active Cardholders Visits Per Week (last 12 weeks)	0.69	0.63	0.06	9.5%
8	No. Card-users in past 4 weeks (average per store)	7,000	6,400	600	9.4%
9	Avg. No. of New Members Per Trading Week	80	60	20	33.3%
10	- Avg. Weekly Inactives	(30)	(25)	(5)	(20.0%)
11	+ Avg. Weekly Reactivated	20	15	5	33.3%
12	= Avg. Weekly Change Per Trading Week	70	50	20	40.0%
13	Active Cardholders at End of Period (avg. per store)	8,500	7,500	1,000	13.3%
14	No. of New Cardholders as % of Beginning Cardholders	0.95%	0.81%	0.14%	17.8%
15	% Cardholders Spending over $30 Per Trading Week	21.40%	19.50%	1.90%	9.7%

Follow-up research can tell us why people shopped only once and what would be necessary to entice them to shop more often. As we gain a greater understanding of our customer behavior, we can change our reward structure for newly joined customers to increase their retention and profitability.

Table 8-6: Cardholders Summary Report

It should now be clear how a deeper understanding of customer behavior, broken down into deciles or quintiles, can assist us not only in changing the way we think about our customers, but also in the way we go to market.

It follows that if customers are central to our business, then key information about them should be part of our monthly top management reporting. The Cardholders Summary Report, Table 8-6, is one suggestion of what might be included in this package.

Table 8-6 shows the results for the latest four weeks for this year and the corresponding period last year. The report is self-explanatory in light of the five previous tables. The purpose of this report is to provide top management with critical information about customers, the foundation of our business.

Beyond the six reports

Although the six tables are suggested as your initial reports, the questions one can (and does) ask about one's customers are endless. Assuming that your customer information is in a relational database, which is common, you can ask all sorts of questions. The answers should come reasonably quickly, but this depends, of course, on the size of your database and the power of your computer.

The more a company delves into its customer data and uses this newfound knowledge to refine its marketing, the more it depends on customer understanding to run its business. This generally means that shortly after you embrace differentiated marketing, you will appoint at least one full-time person to handle the ever increasing number of customer queries. Even the smallest of companies, some of which are the most advanced in the world when it comes to understanding and using customer information, have added such a person.

More information from your database

To illustrate some of the other information being drawn from customer databases, here are some examples:

• *Same household sales.* Some retailers are moving beyond same-store sales as a basic performance benchmark. They are now analyzing their *same-household sales by customer segment.* In particular, they are monitoring which segments are increasing their same-household sales and which are decreasing. They are tracking the same-household activity of their highest spending customers.

• *Gross margin return on customer (GMROC).* This measure is replacing gross margin return on investment (GMROI) as a primary measurement. Given the population growth in the United States during this decade of only 1% annually (continuing a downward decline from previous decades), the proliferation of alternative formats and shopping options, and the continued store growth of retailers, it's easy to see that today there are fewer customers per store than ten years ago. Customers are becoming our limiting factor. Therefore, measuring profitability on a per-customer basis allows us to see our results in terms of the limiting factor. This doesn't say that GMROI is unimportant, but that GMROC is now becoming more important.

- *Direct customer profitability.* With the increasing power of computers, item cost files are beginning to be married to customer data so that retailers can now measure gross profit by customer, both per transaction and over time. The next step will be to deduct the standard variable costs appropriate to each transaction to show each customer's direct customer profitability. This will provide a more accurate measure for making marketing decisions.
- *New store impact.* A variation of the Quo Vadis report has been used to measure the impact that the opening of a new store has on other stores nearby. Retailers are now beginning to track not only which customers went to the new store's grand opening but also who switched their weekly shopping to it.
- *Promotional analysis.* Some retailers are finding great value in analyzing which customers are buying the items in their newspaper advertisements. For example, if soda is promoted below cost and a large number of cases are sold, we have traditionally thought that this was a good promotion because it made a lot of customers happy. However, retailers using their customer database are finding that this is not necessarily so. Too often, they are finding that a small core group of customers (who are *not* in the high spending deciles) are buying large quantities of these deeply discounted promotional items. In other words, these retailers are discovering that such aggressively priced promotions are often misguided because the items are not being purchased in significant amounts by their best customers. And further, the customers who do buy these hotly priced items are not converting into regular profitable customers after the promotions.
- *Customer closeness.* The managers of a number of stores are now finding and meeting the top centile (top one percent) of their customer database. Tim Franklin, a

store manager at Alabama-based Gregerson's Foods, started carrying a list of his top 200 customers. Within six weeks, he had met and learned the names and faces of 192 of them! Not only does this make good business sense but it provides much richer job satisfaction.

Our new retail compass

For decades, we retailers have professed that we were customer driven. These new customer reports now provide us with a compass to help us measure our success in accomplishing this goal. They also demonstrate how inadequate our traditional measurement systems have been in tracking and understanding our customers; and how unsuccessful we have been in changing the behavior of our various customer groups. Fortunately, those days are behind us. We can now measure actual behavior rather than presumed, apparent, or average behavior. We can, at last, understand the numbers behind the numbers!

When appropriate, a finance professor at the Harvard Business School used to quote to his students Professor Finangle's Law:

> *The information we have is not what we want.*
> *The information we want is not what we need.*
> *The information we need is not available.*

Well, the information we need is now available! The race is on to mine this information and to sift from it all of the gold possible.

9

Customer management

One logical development that comes from customer specific marketing is to organize our business around different groups of customers rather than around different groups of products. Appointing managers with full accountability for different customer segments is now possible because the appropriate information is readily obtainable from our customer database. One food retailer has already restructured his marketing efforts around customer segments and reports excellent gains—not just in profits but in a deeper understanding of his customers.

This change is both similar to and different from the development of product category managers over the past decade. It is similar in that it breaks down customers (like products) into segments with a business plan written for each segment (with its unique characteristics), and charges each segment's manager with the accomplishment of the plan's goals.

It is different in that product category management was simply a fragmentation into sub-departments of the existing product-based department structure, whereas customer category management cuts across all departments. It turns the organization structure 90°. It focuses on managing the driver of the business—the customer—regardless of what she buys or in what department she buys it. *It moves our management focus towards the demand side of retailing and away from the supply, or product, side.*

Again, the change is triggered by the changes in technology. Retailers have historically been supply-side-driven, primarily because this was the side of the business for which we had information. Initially, manufacturers supplied retailers with details of the individual items they purchased. Then, the introduction of scanning twenty years ago enabled retailers to gather and analyze their own individual product movement. It was scanning that permitted the development of product category management.

Now at long last, with frequent-shopper cards being read by the same scanners, we are able to apply the same intense scrutiny and management skills to our customers. But to take full advantage of this wonderful new opportunity and move to this next level of marketing sophistication requires a change in our traditional organization structure.

A simple customer segmentation

One simple way to begin customer management is to divide customers into different groups based on their average weekly spending. For example, a simple customer segmentation is:

- *Diamonds:* All customers who spend over $50 per week.
- *Rubies:* All customers who spend between $20 and $50 per week.
- *Opals:* All customers who spend under $20 per week.
- *Nuggets:* All new customers.

The customers comprising the first three segments can be determined at the beginning of each year based upon their performance in the previous year. New customers added during the year can be transferred after a qualifying period to the appropriate other segments (*Diamonds, Rubies, Opals*) at regular intervals.

Economic, not demographic, segmentation

The above groupings are economic-based rather than demographic-based because it is a more logical basis for classifying customers of food retailers.

The economic approach divides customers into segments based on how much they spend each week. This is similar to the segmentation approach of airline frequent-flyer programs in which customer categorization is based on their miles flown. The more they fly, the more they are rewarded. Very frequent flyers on USAir, for example, are classified as either Priority Gold or Priority Gold Plus. Each of these customer categories is managed separately with different reward packages, the goal being to optimize customer profitability.

Segmenting by economics is more appropriate for retailers because as shown in an earlier chapter, customer profit and retention characteristics are directly related to average weekly spending. However, within each economic segment the customer category manager can, should he wish, further sub-segment by demographic characteristic and/or by the *recency* and *frequency* factors, as described earlier.

Demographic segmentation, by comparison, classifies customers by such criteria as where they live, income level, age, ethnic grouping, or family size. Typical demographic customer segments include such well-known terms as Blue Collar, Upper Income, Middle Class Suburban, and Seniors.

Demographics are not recommended as the primary segmentation basis for food retailers because we have not found it to have a strong correlation to profitability. The spending and profitability of senior customers, for example, an important demographic segment, can range from very high to very low.

The customer category manager's responsibility

Each customer category becomes the responsibility of an executive, the *customer category manager*. This position is similar to that of the product category manager found in many retail companies today except, of course, the focus is on optimizing customer, rather than product, results.

Each customer category manager concentrates in the short term on increasing his customers' profit contribution and in the long term on optimizing the *capitalized value of the customers (CVC)* for which he is responsible.

The *capitalized value of customers* is a variation of the Life Time Value (LTV) measure used by direct marketers (which measures the net present value of *new* customers over the next five years). In contrast, the CVC is the net present value of *all* customers, broken down by customer category, with no time limit. Now that we can measure the defection rates of customers by category (as in Table 8-4), *we can quantify the full lifetime value of each of our customer segments.* This approach is similar to the way investment managers capitalize by business unit a company's future earnings stream in order to determine its fair stock price.

What we are doing with customer management is creating a set of customer-based departments, as opposed to product-based departments, with each customer category manager being responsible for:

- the number of customers added to and lost from his customer portfolio;
- the change in the number of his profitable and unprofitable customers; and
- their level of profitability.

As it is in the company's best interests to increase the number of profitable, higher-spending customers, the customer managers for Rubies ($20-50 spenders per week) and Opals (under $20) are assessed and rewarded based upon how many of their customers move to a higher segment. The manager of the Diamonds category (over $50 per week) is rewarded for how long he can retain these prime customers.

Likewise, the Nuggets manager is rewarded for the number of active, profitable *new* customers promoted to the other three categories. Furthermore, he is not rewarded for the number of customers who apply for a card, but for the number of *profitable* new customers he can attract, and more critically, *retain*, for the company.

The 7 ways to improve profits

From a customer-centered view of the world, there are seven ways to improve profits, all of which are now measurable. When practicing customer management, retailers will focus on all seven:

1) *Add more new profitable customers.*
2) *Add fewer new unprofitable customers.*
3) *Lose fewer existing profitable customers.*
4) *Increase the average life of profitable customers.*
5) *Increase the conversion rate of unprofitable customers to profitability, or increase their defection rates.*
6) *Increase the profitability of all profitable customers.*
7) *Decrease the unprofitability of unprofitable customers.*

With the exception of the first two options, each will become a quantifiable objective of the Diamond, Ruby, and Opal customer managers.

Advantages of customer category management

One towering advantage the new customer category manager has over today's product category manager is that he is dealing directly with the customer. He knows her activity and profitability profile and can continuously modify her offer-bundle to encourage her in the direction that will help accomplish his goals.

Another powerful advantage is that it makes the setting of product priorities easier. In other words, armed with customer information, the retailer can determine product selection and space allocation by *who* is buying the products. For example, one store manager, whose store was over-trading, wanted to rationalize his store layout. He looked at the forty feet of shelf space allocated to candy. It had good sales figures, but what was the *correct* candy space allocation? Delving into his customer database and looking at his category movement by customer, he found that his best customers (the top 30% who provided him with 75% of his sales) were not heavy candy buyers. Such customers didn't start appearing until his middle deciles. After further analysis, he cut his candy section to twenty feet and extended his adjacent baby category by the same amount, as his best customers were heavy baby category purchasers. Interestingly, the sales of *both* categories rose after the realignment!

It was a simple case of allocating shelf space based primarily on customer importance and second, on product importance. If we are, as we profess, customer-centered retailers, then this is the correct ordering of our priorities.

This example also highlights that customer management is not meant to replace product category management, but needs to be integrated with it. I expect that we will see customer category managers working in a matrix-type relationship with product category managers. However, the ultimate responsibility for profitability will rest with the customer category manager.

Customer management is already in practice

Even though retailers are still breaking new ground in their thought processes on this subject, it has moved past the theoretical stage. One leading differentiated retailer is already an ardent practitioner of customer management. His company charges out its weekly marketing costs (mailers, markdowns, and other direct costs) to each of its *customer categories,* allowing him to measure the effects of his marketing efforts on the sales and profitability of each category. Each category's marketing efforts are then continually refined with different levels of prices, promotions, and other rewards.

In addition, each week he measures his performance, not on a year-to-year, same-store basis but on a year-to-year, same-household basis. His company is very close to running entirely on Direct Customer Profitability, as opposed to Direct Product Profitability.

Systematically measuring progress

As we begin marketing to our different customer segments with offers appropriate to each segment, a systematic way to keep track of our successes and failures is needed. One company that excels in this area is Tennessee-based Service Merchandise. According to Deborah Lowman, Vice President of Marketing, every major marketing initiative is subsequently reviewed, and a report is written addressing four major areas:

1) Results. What were the financial results of this program? (These are recorded in a standard format for inter-program comparisons.)

2) Lessons. What were the major lessons learned from this program? (For example, our *10%-off* offer had stronger pulling power than a *$10-off* offer.)

3) Recommendations for next year. If we run this program again next year, what recommendations do we have, based on our experiences with this initiative?

4) *Spin-offs.* What ideas did we gain from this initiative that we can spin off and use in programs for other categories or products?

As you can imagine, a library of such reports built up over time becomes an invaluable marketing asset.

Integrate customer management

Customer management should also be integrated with the operational side of the company. One retailer already holds his store department managers accountable for customer additions to and defections from their respective departments. He has found, for example, that customers may stop shopping a particular department, yet still shop in other departments. Therefore, he now holds departmental managers accountable for such defections. One obvious side-benefit of this is that it makes all departments more customer-oriented, as they now have a scorecard (their customer defection reports) to measure their customer satisfaction abilities.

Customer categories are not completely independent of one another as some programs cut across all segments. For example, all customers with pets may be targeted with special offers, regardless of how much they spend in total. In these *sub-club programs*, as they are known, either the identical offer can be made to all customers, or the basic offer can be modified according to which customer category the pet owner belongs.

New measurements

As was the case with product category management, a new set of measurements is required with this new customer emphasis. In addition to the *capitalized value of cus-*

tomers calculation mentioned earlier, a *customer flow report* is very helpful. This records the flow of customers into the company (and into which categories they flow), the internal movement of customers among these customer categories, and the customer outflows. Such an insight into your customer dynamics is essential if you wish to monitor and influence customer behavior.

At the end of this chapter the Customer Category Performance Report (Table 9-1) is presented as one approach to show top management the contribution of each customer category.

How to read the Customer Category Report

For simplicity, the twelve-week report in Table 9-1 was prepared for a single store. The first page displays the composition of sales and gross profits by the four customer categories described earlier, together with the unidentified transactions (those transactions that are not card-based). The report clearly shows the significantly different contributions of the different customer segments together with their changes from last year.

Pages 2 and 3 of the report show the sales components, both by week and by segment, that are behind the totals on page 1. And on page 4 the numbers of currently active Diamond, Ruby, Opal, and Nugget customers are logged. In addition, page 4 shows each segment's year-to-year defection rates (lines 50-54), the number of new cardholders (line 55), and the number of new customers expressed as a percentage of the active customer base (line 56).

The two middle columns of Table 9-1 provide comparisons of this year with the same period last year, while the right-hand columns (with the exception of the Gross Profit section) show in percentage terms either what each category comprises of the total or how it varies from the average category performance.

Table 9-1 is similar to the traditional departmental reporting of retailers—but with customer-based, instead of product-based, departments, providing a much richer depth of understanding of the underlying activity of our business.

Expanding the boundaries

The emergence of customer management is a huge stride forward for retailers because it allows us to deal directly with our customers, rather than indirectly, as in the past, through our products. We can now build our whole business around disparate groups of customers— market to them, measure their responses, understand their dynamics and economics, and then, with this new knowledge, market to them even more effectively. We can offer different combinations of prices and benefits to each customer segment, allowing us to expand even further the boundaries that product category management previously added to our industry knowledge.

Customer Category Performance Report

XYZ Stores Inc. **Table 9 - 1**

For 12 weeks ending 12/31/99

		Results		TY Better (Worse)			% Total	
Latest 12 Week Sales (Total)		TY	LY	#	%		TY	LY
1 Diamond (SPW > $50)	$k	1,500	1,300	200	15.4%		51.0%	47.6%
2 Ruby (SPW > $20-50)	$k	1,200	1,000	200	20.0%		40.8%	36.6%
3 Opal (SPW < $20)	$k	200	400	(200)	(50.0%)		6.8%	14.6%
4 Nugget (New in Latest 12 Wks)	$k	40	32	8	25.0%		1.4%	1.2%
5 Total Active Cardholders	$k	2,940	2,732	208	7.6%		81.7%	82.8%
6 Unidentified Transactions	$k	660	568	92	16.2%		18.3%	17.2%
7 Total	$k	3,600	3,300	300	9.1%		100.0%	100.0%
Latest 12 Weeks Gross Profit (Total)							**Gross Profit %**	
8 Diamond (SPW > $50)	$k	350.0	310.0	40.0	12.9%		23.33	23.85
9 Ruby (SPW > $20-50)	$k	260.0	220.0	40.0	18.2%		21.67	22.00
10 Opal (SPW < $20)	$k	50.0	70.0	(20.0)	(28.6%)		25.00	17.50
11 Nugget (New in Latest 12 Wks)	$k	8.4	7.5	0.9	12.0%		21.00	23.44
12 Total Active Cardholders	$k	668.4	607.5	60.9	10.0%		22.73	22.24
13 Unidentified Transactions	$k	159.6	132.5	27.1	20.5%		24.18	23.33
14 Total	$k	828.0	740.0	88.0	11.9%		23.00	22.42

Sales Per Trading Week		Results		TY Better (Worse)		% Total	
		TY	LY	#	%	TY	LY
15 Diamond (SPW > $50)	$	125,000	108,333	16,667	15.4%	51.0%	47.6%
16 Ruby (SPW > $20-50)	$	100,000	83,333	16,667	20.0%	40.8%	36.6%
17 Opal (SPW < $20)	$	16,667	33,333	(16,667)	(50.0%)	6.8%	14.6%
18 Nugget (New in Latest 12 Wks)	$	3,333	2,667	667	25.0%	1.4%	1.2%
19 Total Active Cardholders	$	245,000	227,667	17,333	7.6%	81.7%	82.8%
20 Unidentified Transactions	$	55,000	47,333	7,667	16.2%	18.3%	17.2%
21 Total	$	300,000	275,000	25,000	9.1%	100.0%	100.0%

Customer Spending Per Week		Results		TY Better (Worse)		Var. from Avg.	
		TY	LY	#	%	TY	LY
22 Diamond (SPW > $50)	$	59.52	57.02	2.51	4.4%	206.1%	198.0%
23 Ruby (SPW > $20-50)	$	25.00	23.15	1.85	8.0%	28.6%	21.0%
24 Opal (SPW <$20)	$	3.09	6.06	(2.97)	(49.1%)	(84.1%)	(68.3%)
25 Nugget (New in Latest 12 Wks)	$	3.03	2.96	0.07	2.3%	(84.4%)	(84.5%)
26 Total Active Cardholders	$	19.44	19.13	0.31	1.6%	18.4%	28.3%
27 Unidentified Transactions	$	9.71	7.24	2.47	34.1%	(40.9%)	(51.5%)
28 Total	$	16.42	14.91	1.51	10.1%	0.0%	0.0%

	Visits Per Week		Results		TY Better (Worse)		Var. from Avg.	
			TY	LY	#	%	TY	LY
29	Diamond (SPW > $50)	#	1.11	1.10	0.01	1.3%	51.4%	57.4%
30	Ruby (SPW > $20-50)	#	0.79	0.81	(0.02)	(2.3%)	7.8%	16.3%
31	Opal (SPW < $20)	#	0.66	0.58	0.08	13.9%	(10.7%)	(17.4%)
32	Nugget (New in Latest 12 Wks)	#	0.19	0.14	0.05	36.4%	(74.2%)	(80.1%)
33	Total Active Cardholders	#	0.73	0.70	0.04	5.4%	(10.1%)	(13.4%)
34	Unidentified Transactions	#	1.00	1.00	0.00	0.0%	22.5%	24.3%
35	Total	#	0.82	0.80	0.01	1.5%	0.0%	0.0%
	Spending Per Visit							
36	Diamond (SPW > $50)	$	53.57	52.00	1.57	3.0%	102.3%	89.4%
37	Ruby (SPW > $20-50)	$	31.58	28.57	3.01	10.5%	19.2%	4.1%
38	Opal (SPW < $20)	$	4.71	10.53	(5.82)	(55.3%)	(82.2%)	(61.7%)
39	Nugget (New in Latest 12 Wks)	$	16.00	21.33	(5.33)	(25.0%)	(39.6%)	(22.3%)
40	Total Active Cardholders	$	26.49	27.46	(0.97)	(3.5%)	31.7%	48.1%
41	Unidentified Transactions	$	9.71	7.24	2.47	34.1%	(51.7%)	(61.0%)
42	Total	$	20.11	18.54	1.57	8.5%	0.0%	0.0%

Customers Per Store			Results		TY Better (Worse)		% Total	
			TY	LY	#	%	TY	LY
43	Diamond (SPW > $50)	#	2,100	1,900	200	10.5%	21.0%	19.0%
44	Ruby (SPW > $20-50)	#	4,000	3,600	400	11.1%	39.0%	38.0%
45	Opal (SPW < $20)	#	5,400	5,500	(100)	(1.8%)	32.0%	33.0%
46	Nugget (New in Latest 12 Wks)	#	1,100	900	200	22.2%	8.0%	10.0%
47	Total Active Cardholders	#	12,600	11,900	700	5.9%	69.0%	64.5%
48	Unidentified Transactions	#	5,667	6,542	(875)	(13.4%)	31.0%	35.5%
49	Total	#	18,267	18,442	(175)	(.9%)	100.0%	100.0%
	Other Key Information							
50	Def. Rate Last Year's Diamond	%	4.3%	8.7%	(4.4%)	50.6%		
51	Def. Rate Last Year's Ruby	%	27.1%	30.2%	(3.1%)	10.3%		
52	Def. Rate Last Year's Opal	%	53.9%	51.3%	2.6%	(5.1%)		
53	Def. Rate Last Year's Nugget	%	44.4%	53.8%	(9.4%)	17.5%		
54	Def. Rate Last Year's Total	%	19.8%	30.3%	(10.5%)	34.7%		
55	New CH (avg. per trading week)	#	92	75	17	22.2%		
56	New CH as % of All Or. Active CH	%	0.80%	0.68%	0.12%	16.9%		

Part V: Implementation

The goal of this section is to assist in your transition to *customer specific marketing.*

Chapter 10 sets forth the key issues involved in getting started.

Chapter 11 gives some guidance in going the distance after the first six months.

10

Getting started

The transition to customer specific marketing is not just a matter of turning on a switch! There is no canned package you can buy off the shelf to make you a leading practitioner and hike your profits overnight. We are dealing with a dramatic break from our traditional marketing practices. If the change is poorly executed, you may be hobbled with a layer of added costs rather than be basking in the sunshine of increased profits. This chapter is intended to help you down the second path.

The three phases

The transition to customer specific marketing consists of three distinct phases:
- Building the business case
- A successful launch
- Going the distance

This chapter deals with the first two phases. The third phase is covered in Chapter 11.

Building the business case

Before embracing customer specific marketing, a retailer goes through significant investigation, thought, and soul searching. If the tentative conclusion is to proceed, a formal business plan is usually prepared for the Board of Directors, because *it involves a fundamental business change.* It is critical to understand that you are embarking on a major change in your strategy which will impact every part of the organization, as well as significantly change the nature of the relationship with your customers. It will require the understanding, support, and commitment of all employees. The change will be a milestone in the company's history.

A business plan's table of contents, similar to that used by several companies, is shown to assist you in your preparation.

Table of Contents

1) Executive Summary
2) Why move to *Customer Specific Marketing* (CSM)?
    a) The one critical reason
    b) Other reasons and benefits
    c) Limitations and risks
3) The competitive situation
    a) Competitors
    b) Our relative strengths and weaknesses
4) An overview of how CSM works
5) Our objectives for CSM
    a) Customers - Behavior
        - Knowledge
        - Relationships
    b) Sales
    c) Profits
6) Requirements for success
    a) Preparation
    b) Launch
    c) Post launch
    d) Long term
    e) Employees
7) Equipment and software
    a) Current position
    b) Requirements
8) Database
    a) Issues (eg, household linking)

b) What information and for how long
c) Requirements
9) Measurements, benchmarks, and reports
10) Privacy issues
11) Income and cost assumptions
   a) One-time
   b) Ongoing
12) Key dates

The section headings in the table of contents are self-explanatory, and companies prepare each section appropriately to their own circumstances.

Comment, however, should be made on the shortest, but most important part of the plan: identifying the one critical reason why your company should embrace customer specific marketing. The business case is then built around this brief statement. The reason must be simple and easily understood by all employees. Obviously, it's not the same for every company.

One food retailer's *critical reason* was to minimize the sales loss expected from the imminent entry of a major competitor into its marketplace.

This company, which had an extremely successful transition to differentiated marketing with total company-wide commitment, spent a great deal of time communicating the implications of its new marketing strategy. All employees understood that they were going to change the prices on selected items to give regular customers even better pricing than before, while convenience shoppers (who elect not to apply for a free customer card) would pay higher prices. Employees understood that, in this way, the company had the best chance of retaining their regular customers. They also understood that if they were to lose any customers to the new, highly regarded entrant, they would be the lower spending, convenience and occasional customers.

No one in the company doubted that the top officers were committed to differentiated marketing and that it was to become a central part of their business.

A successful launch

The clearer your objectives, the greater your chance of a successful launch. Therefore, in planning your transition to differentiated marketing, one critical factor is deciding what you want to accomplish.

Goals

One company spelled out its goals as follows:

1) *To encourage all customers to become cardholders;*
2) *To encourage cardholders to bring and use their cards on every visit;*
3) *To reward, proportionally, our regular customers;*
4) *To provide a good database of customer information;*
5) *To learn more about what motivates customers;*
6) *To give customers a reason to drive past competitors and shop with us;*
7) *To encourage cardholders to increase their share of spending with us;*
8) *To increase our store sales in the short and long term; and*
9) *To increase our company profitability.*

Another company stated the following objectives of their new marketing strategy:

1) *We will reward, proportionally more, those customers who exhibit greater loyalty (and therefore, generate greater profitability) by introducing a customer card.*
2) *Initially, we will focus on disproportionately rewarding our best customers, who are defined as follows:*
   a) *Cardholders who spend over $360 in a twelve-week quarter (an average of $30 or more a week);*

b) *Cardholders who spend over $1,040 in any rolling 52-week year (at least $20 a week); and*

c) *Cardholders who have spent an average of over $15 a week over the past three years and who have shopped with us in the last twelve weeks.*

3) We will, over time, reward these customers more than others in a variety of ways, including:
   a) *Price (better prices on selected items);*
   b) *Purchases (special rewards based on their total spending);*
   c) *Partners (special benefits when they shop at stores other than our own);*
   d) *Privileges (both pre-announced and surprises); and*
   e) *Participation (special feedback sessions with the goal of improving our offering to this key group in particular).*

4) Over time, we will increase our customer retention and addition rates by taking some of the monies that we, in the past, have given away as markdowns and spent on advertising to everyone. We will re-apply these monies to this specific group to encourage them to be even more loyal.

5) Over time, our card will become synonymous with our brand. We will keep layering value after value around it.

This program, of course, did not mean that other cardholders didn't receive benefits. They did. It's just that this retailer deliberately skewed his reward structure in favor of his higher spending cardholders.

Specific Goals

From these overall objectives, specific goals are then set for the first six months. They should be simple and straightforward, such as:

• **To have 50% of all transactions on the card within twelve weeks** of the card's launch (yielding about 80% of sales). For food retailers who offer free card membership, this goal is readily being achieved, as seen in Table 10-1.

This table shows, by week, the average percentage of all store transactions captured by three food retailers with their newly launched cards. To achieve the strong 28% result in launch week, each company had also conducted two weeks of pre-launch publicity.

Of course, for other retailers, this target should be adjusted for the average customer visitation frequency of their particular industry.

<u>Table 10 - 1</u>
<u>Cardholder Transactions</u>
<u>as Percentage of Total</u>

<u>Week #</u>	<u>% of Total</u> <u>Transactions</u>
1	28%
2	38%
3	40%
4	45%
5	48%
6	50%
7	52%
8	53%
9	53%
10	54%
11	56%
12	56%

- **To have 60% of all transactions on the card within twenty-four weeks** of the card's launch.
- **To significantly cut back print advertising** once 50% of transactions are being captured on the card.
- **To become comfortable with this new way of marketing.** Although this is not a quantifiable goal, it is very important because a number of people (both in and out

of management) experience some difficulty in switching to this new way of marketing.

Card transaction goals are set in numeric terms because it forces management to take the necessary steps to make *customer specific marketing* the core business strategy. The higher the percentage of transactions, the more central it is.

A high percentage of transactions is crucial to your strategy's success because the larger your customer information base, the better your differentiation decisions. Another vital reason is that the larger the share of customers affected by your marketing tactics, the greater the impact of those decisions on your company's profitability.

An early target of 50% of transactions is set out above. This, to me, is the *minimum* requirement for a food retailer to indicate he is serious about customer specific marketing. But understand that this is only the equivalent of a bachelor's degree! More serious students of customer specific marketing are achieving the equivalent of a Master's degree (over 60% of transactions), or a Ph.D. (over 70% of transactions). One food retailer—a true devotee of customer specific marketing whose whole business revolves around his card program—captures over 80% of transactions and over 90% of sales on his card!

As a general rule, the percentage of transactions captured on your card reflects how central the card is to your strategy. The higher the percentage, the more central customer specific marketing is to the business. However, it is fair to point out that lower percentages are appropriate in certain situations, such as tourist areas and other areas of high customer transience, or where a fee is charged for the card, or where there are minimum purchase qualifiers.

Customer Acceptance

Customers must experience the benefits of presenting a card at each transaction to readily welcome the transition to a card-based relationship. A program which combines the following elements usually accomplishes this well:

• *Make joining easy.* Include the application form in your launch advertisement. Have forms easily accessible at a sign-up table when customers enter the store. Keep the form and sign-up process as simple and as brief as possible. And make the program easy to understand. Gerland's Food Fair, in Houston, Texas, has a continuously playing video near each store's entrance describing their Customer Advantage card. Chief Operating Officer Kevin Doris explains that he wants all new customers to understand the program.

• *Feature in launch week at least 25% of your advertised specials as cardholders' specials only.* During the following eight to ten weeks, increase this share to at least 80% of your advertised specials.

• *Convert at least 25% of your regular Temporary Price Reductions to cardholder specials in launch week.* During the following eight to ten weeks convert the balance of all items featured as TPR's to cardholder specials only.

• *Increase/decrease at least thirty image and private label items.* Increase their regular shelf prices by, say, 5-10% for non-cardholders while, at the same time, lowering the cardholders' price for these same items by 5-10%. Over time, enlarge this list.

If you follow the above guidelines, customers will experience the benefits of membership immediately. However, some will ask the question, "Why do I have to use a card now to get these specials, when I didn't have to before?"

As your answer should be, "Because we want to reward our regular customers more," you must start demonstrating this immediately. This is often done in one of two ways:

1) Introduce, either at launch or as soon as possible afterwards, a sweepstakes program with some attractive prizes, with cardholders automatically entered when they use their card.

2) As early as the third or fourth week after launch week, announce a special twelve-week program during which customers' total spending will be rewarded. For example, offer a 5% *off your next purchase* gift certificate to cardholders who spend more than $250 in the twelve-week period, and a *10% off* certificate to those who spend over $500.

Both the sweepstakes and the gift certificate program obviously reward your regular customers more favorably than your casual and irregular shoppers, thereby signaling that you are serious about favoring those who regularly shop with you.

Program elimination

The launch of your differentiated marketing program is usually the time to withdraw a number of your existing marketing offers—programs such as meeting competitors' ad items, honoring competitors' coupons, offering across-the-board category discounts, manager's specials, and in-store specials. Some companies also have successfully eliminated their double coupon and senior citizens' discount programs at this time.

When the reasons and benefits of the marketing switch are simple and clearly communicated, the transition is usually quite smooth. Yes, a few customers will complain. However, these complaints are seldom, if ever, from your best customers. Typically, they come from those at the other end of the customer spectrum!

What's the best program?

No one differentiated marketing program is best. What is optimal for your company depends a great deal on whether you are first, second, third, or last in the marketplace with your program.

If you are not first in your market area with customer specific marketing, it's usually best to focus on developing an approach *different* from the others. Your objective is to differentiate your offer—to force customers to choose where they shop. This means deciding what is the best appeal for that customer segment on which you plan to concentrate. It's preferable to aim at one primary customer segment rather than developing a program that appeals to all segments. Trying to please everybody usually pleases nobody—except your competitors!

Rewards, not inducements

There is no need to offer customers a special inducement simply to complete an application form, such as a free item or 5% off your initial purchase. Customers will readily join your program if the benefits are obvious and immediate. It's better for customers to *experience* your program's benefits and special prices during their sign-up visit than to receive a reward for filling out an application form.

Employee rewards

Similarly, it's preferable not to reward cashiers for the number of application forms they have customers complete. The whole store team should be talking to customers about the advantages of membership, based upon the benefits they have already experienced with their cards. For this reason, some companies invest in programs providing additional rewards for employees who regularly use their cards. The more employees use their cards, the more benefits they receive, and the more they understand the program. And the more they experience and understand it, the stronger the believers they become—which means that they are out on the shop floor enthusiastically singing the program's praises to customers and fellow employees alike. These additional employee benefits are, in effect, an indirect training and selling cost of the program.

Two current practices that accomplish these objectives include:

- A discount on employee card purchases, over and above the deals regular customers receive. For example, employees receive a *10% off their next purchase* gift certificate each time their accumulated spending reaches a multiple of $250.
- A sweepstakes for employees only, with a quarterly prize of the employee's average weekly wages for that quarter (with a $100 minimum). Each employee receives one sweepstakes entry for each week in the quarter in which his card recorded at least $25 of spending.

Employee involvement

As employee enthusiasm and understanding of this new marketing program is paramount, many companies quietly begin their program several weeks before the public launch, opening it just for employees (and insome cases selected customers). This allows employees to become familiar with the changes involved in this new marketing approach, to recognize its benefits, and to understand how it favors the company's regular customers. And of course the company gains from their feedback before the program is publicly launched.

For maximum employee understanding, keep it simple. One helpful rule of thumb is that any part-time employee, within half an hour of being on the store floor, should be able to answer any customer question about the program. No aspect of this program should be so complicated that a customer has to be redirected to the service desk to have her question answered.

After the launch, keep your employees aware of how the program is progressing. In particular, they should know their store's percentage of card-based to total transactions. Later, as soon as the relevant information becomes available, employees should also know how effective they are at retaining their customers and how their performance compares to other stores. Such information, of course, is powerful feedback to a store team.

From the customer's perspective

Besides thinking of the issues from the employee's perspective, we should look at them through the customer's eyes. For example, it's easier to remember the starting and ending dates of a sweepstakes as the first and last day of a calendar month than the starting and ending dates of the company's four-week accounting period (which is often how retailers offer such programs today). Likewise, rewards based on purchases over a twelve-week period are better offered over three consecutive calendar months.

The same line of thinking should also be applied to your markdown policy. Because the average Sunday newspaper coupon is over $0.50, to achieve any serious impact, your featured savings should be at least $0.30, or 20% of the regular selling price, whichever is less. Further, rounding the customer's savings to the nearest $0.10 is more in synch with our coupon age. For example, a $0.30 savings is easier to grasp than either $0.29 or $0.32. When, after all, was the last time you opened your Sunday paper and found coupons for such odd amounts?

During the first six months of the program, because of the great value of advertised cardholder specials, limits are often placed on them. Where this is done, to make it easy for customers, apply the *same* limit (eg, limit of two, four, or five items) in those weeks that you feature limits. Varying purchase limits in the same week just makes shopping unnecessarily more complicated for customers.

Cards

Given the high defection rate of new cardholders, some companies issue thin, temporary membership cards in an effort to cut costs. Then only when a new cardholder reaches a certain threshold (for example, accumulated spending of $250 or making their third visit within six weeks of their first transaction) does the company issue a better quality, permanent membership card.

One popular alternative to both temporary and regular credit card-style membership cards is a *key tag card*. These cards, with a hole in one end, are about half the size of a credit card. The customer simply slips this key tag card onto her key ring which, of course, she has with her when she shops. Not only does this mean that a customer never forgets to bring her card, but it helps in your fight for wallet space, a problem given the proliferation of cards offered to customers today. The key tag also acts as an advertisement for your company. Furthermore, most retailers offer a *free key-return service* if the keys are ever lost and the finder drops them into a mailbox. (On the back of their key tag cards is a guaranteed return service, courtesy of the retailer.) Each store typically receives one set of lost keys from the Post Office to return to its rightful owner every one to two weeks! Thus, this service becomes yet another benefit of belonging to your card program.

Privacy

Privacy is a fascinating issue as it relates to food retailers. Possibly because of the range of products they buy, many people feel very sensitive about their transactions being captured in great detail by their "grocer." In comparison, credit card companies and direct marketers have extensive databases on these same people with a wealth of information on their incomes and purchasing habits.

Yet, to date, customers have had less to fear from their food retailer. I have been extremely impressed with the responsibility of the food industry and its approach to customer privacy. I know of no food retailer who sells customer information to any outside party. That, of course, cannot be said of other business sectors.

Typical of retailers' concerns for their customers' privacy is the following statement found on a membership application for the Ukrop's program:

By signing here, I ask that a Ukrop's Valued Customer Card be issued as I have requested. I agree to allow Ukrop's and their data processing suppliers to record and make use of the information about the products I purchase. I would also like to receive valuable savings and special information by mail from Ukrop's and packaged goods manufacturers.

[Then there is a space for the customer to sign and date. This is followed by another statement:]

Since your purchases will be automatically recorded, we will be able to provide you with special offers and information about items that may be of interest to you—both from our stores and from our carefully screened companies. If you wish to receive only the monthly mailing from Ukrop's, please check this box.

The above demonstrates a keen sensitivity towards customers' privacy. Retailers such as Ukrop's may send mailings and special offers to customers from manufacturers, but Ukrop's will *never* give manufacturers or any other party the names and addresses of their customers. This level of responsibility is common in the food industry.

Another interesting observation is that customers' concerns about privacy appear to be in inverse proportion to the benefits received. The greater the value associated with the card, the less customers seem to raise the privacy issue.

Retailers and manufacturers

Rather than going to the manufacturing community prior to the launch of their differentiated marketing program, many retailers hold back and simply convert the promotional deals already negotiated to card-based promotions. Then, once the program has been up and running for at least four weeks, retailers often invite their suppliers to attend one of a series of brief (about one hour) meetings. During these presentations, the retailer describes the nature and objectives of his new marketing strategy, the early results, and the changes that he would like to see in his company's relationship with suppliers. Retailers have found that it is easier to explain what changes are required in the supplier-retailer relationship after both sides have had a chance to see differentiated marketing in practice.

Technology

It is, of course, very easy to become enthused about the myriad offer-bundles possible with differentiated marketing. Remember, however, that all of these changes are a function of technology. Unfortunately, this is the area where the biggest frustrations occur when exploring the possibility of converting to differentiated marketing. The problems retailers typically confront include:

- Their point-of-sale equipment is provided by different vendors.
- Their point-of-sale equipment is not of the same generation and, therefore, has different capabilities.
- Systems connectivity problems limit what they can do.
- Their particular brand of point-of-sale equipment does not have the same offer flexibility as their competitors'.

For some companies, the cost of replacing or upgrading their point-of-sale equipment appears so high thatswitching to differentiated marketing seems prohibitively costly. Of course, it could easily be argued that standing still will be even more costly to the company's long-term future!

When evaluating the capabilities of your front-end systems for differentiated marketing, some basic questions that should be asked include:

- How many different pricing tiers can we have for each product? Five or more?
- Can our system process random weights at the regular price as well as at a special cardholder price? (This is particularly important as you will want to include all departments in the program.)
- Can our system readily accept limits of varying quantities on different cardholder items?
- Will our system permit tiered-pricing, where the price to the customer is a function of the total order size?
- Will it allow multi-buys for cardholders? (For example, *buy three, get the fourth one free.*)
- Will it process the mixing-and-matching of flavors? (For example, can cardholders buy any three flavors of Jell-O for one price?)

- Will it process mix-and-match products? (For example, buy spaghetti at full price and receive the spaghetti sauce at half price.)
- Can time limits be imposed on offers to cardholders? (For example, can offers on individual items be made to cardholders for varying periods from, say, three hours to a week?)
- Will the system process double or triple coupons, up to a certain quantity, for cardholders only? Will it allow the quantity of coupons to be a function of the amount of purchases in, say, the previous month?
- Will the system allow a points program?
- Will the points program be on-line company-wide or will each store stand alone (with information updated as of the previous evening)?

The three major point-of-sale equipment vendors in the United States, IBM, ICL/Fujitsu, and NCR, have varying capabilities in answer to the above questions. Therefore, retailers considering replacing their current point-of-sale equipment should develop a checklist, using the questions above as a base, and they should test it against the major vendors and against several of the newly emerging, smaller companies. Two such companies which have developed state-of-the-art front-end systems with a full open architecture base are in Pennsylvania: Bristol-based SASI (215-785-4321) and Coraopolis-based EPS (800-377-2005). Both of these companies see customer specific marketing as the heart of retailing in the future and have developed hardware and systems to satisfy these newly emerging needs. Two other front-end systems companies with similar ambitions that are worthy of your consideration are Innovax (214-550-8371) and ACR Systems (904-296-8554). This isn't the end of the list, of course, but it will set you on the right path.

Because of the fast-changing nature of this field, new developments are frequently announced. A regular updating from the above companies and others is strongly recommended. This will help you understand not just your position on the technological ability scale, but also how your competitors may change the competitive dynamics if they install more sophisticated equipment than you. *Retailing has undoubtedly entered a new era of electronic marketing, and just as in warfare, those with the most technologically advanced weapons have a decided advantage.*

In a like vein, software is continuously being developed to assist retailers in mining their customer database, running regular reports, and answering specific queries on all sorts of issues. Again, because of the newness of this way of retail marketing, the software programs offered still leave much to be desired and, like point-of-sale equipment, this area should be regularly reviewed.

All of the major POS-equipment vendors either offer their own database software for customer use or have alliances with specialty database houses which they recommend to potential clients. As mentioned earlier, two independent companies with excellent database software are RMS and S2 Systems.

When evaluating the capabilities of a retail database vendor, a few key questions include:

- What standard reports are produced?

- How long does it take to produce them?

- Which reports have drill-down capability?

- How user friendly is the query capability feature?

- What enhancements are being planned?

- Who are some of the existing users that I may contact to learn of their experiences with your software?

Why some transitions fail

Where top management commitment is clear and obvious, success is largely assured. When top management is not directly involved in the transformation, or when they adopt a half-hearted, wait-and-see attitude, customer specific marketing is more likely to fail. As, alas, it does too often.

Based upon my observations of unsuccessful programs, other reasons for failure include:

• *Timidity.* Top management is not committed to the change. The highest level of management doesn't have a champion pushing the program. The result is that the company as a whole doesn't stand behind it—some departments do, some don't. What usually results is that the company captures about 25-35% of the transactions (about 50-60% of sales) on the card. No noticeable profit gain comes from the program. In fact, with such results the program is most probably costing money, which leads to even more timidity and indecision. In this situation, management becomes apprehensive about increasing the number of exclusive cardholders' specials, fearful of losing sales from non-cardholders. They become paralyzed in no-man's land, and the program begins to stagnate and die.

• *Non-core.* Customer specific marketing does not become the core of the company's strategy. The card program is launched, but few, if any, of the existing marketing practices are withdrawn. The new initiative simply becomes yet another promotional program.

• *Non-differentiated.* The best and least valuable customers are *insufficiently* differentiated. Management is reluctant to withdraw rewards from one group of customers while increasing them to others.

• *Puny rewards.* The store electronic discounts are not meaningful. One company offered hundreds of savings of $0.05-0.20 per item. Cardholders were underwhelmed when they saw how minuscule the total of their cardholder savings was and saw little reason to keep presenting their cards.

• *Confusing message.* The launch message was very confusing. In spite of a wide range of customer communications, customers' perceptions of the new program were quite different from the reality. In one case, customers thought that the newly announced program was going to give them an across-the-board discount on all purchases and that the program would eliminate the need for them to clip manufacturer's coupons. Neither perception was correct.

• *Over-reliance on vendors.* The retailer thinks that this is a program in which all the markdowns can be simply transferred to the vendors, coupled with a transaction fee. In one case where this occurred, vendors did concur, but gave price concessions (and a transaction fee) on their slower moving products only. This, of course, did not generate the customer excitement necessary for success.

• *Information starvation.* Some companies used their card program simply as a shelf electronic discount mechanism. They didn't keep files on their customers or track their activity. They overlooked the fact that the real value of differentiated marketing lies in its information.

• *Weak operation.* Programs built on quicksand don't do well. Some companies have thought that differentiated marketing would solve all their problems. Of course, this is a fallacy. Simply launching a card program will not overcome a retailer's inherent operational and marketing problems. It will not overcome the problems arising from poor customer service, dirty floors, or disappointing housekeeping. *Customer specific marketing is a tie-breaker, not a miracle worker!*

A personal experience made this very clear to me. In our town, we have a number of book stores. I pay a $10 annual membership fee to two of them in exchange for a 10% discount on my purchases, along with some other benefits. Yet I now find, with the opening of a third major book store, which does not have a card program with membership discounts, that I shop there regularly because of its better selection of business books. In addition, it has the best selection of children's books, which my daughter prefers. In this case, for me, a good selection takes precedence over a membership discount program.

• *Internal political problems.* Internal problems, including turf-protection and foot-dragging, seem to increase in proportion to the size of the organization. In the absence of strong top management leadership regarding differentiated marketing, one often finds that the larger the company, the greater the resistance to change as the princes of the organization defend their organizational castles. As one executive of a large retailer explained, it took three years for their merchandisers, vendors, and store employees to really "get" the program. The executive described the following cycle:

First Year. Open resistance from merchandisers, vendors, and store employees who did not fully understand the program. Top management support was absolutely vital during that first year.

Second Year. The year of quiet sabotage. The unbelievers worked behind the scenes to kill the program.

Third Year. Acceptance—at last! By now there was enough proof for everyone to get behind the program. The merchandisers, after several years of resistance, started talking to vendors about "their program." They now claimed to be its proud parent!

Most companies will go through some combination of overt and covert resistance. Expect it and plan to minimize it. This is yet another reason why it is critical for top management, including the board of directors, to understand the magnitude of the change in thinking that comes with differentiated marketing. It is also critical for them to endorse and champion the necessary changes openly, because without this support success is uncertain and many of the rewards will go unrealized.

Retail is detail

The axiom *retail is detail* rings true once again as we think through the innumerable details involved in the transition to differentiated marketing. Many factors must be considered including ensuring an easy transition from the customer's perspective, nurturing and maintaining employee enthusiasm, and sorting out and handling the technological transition. It requires the drawing together of resources from all parts of your organization. The transition is not just a function of the marketing department—it touches on, and involves, every part of your company, starting at the very top of the company.

Furthermore, the issues raised in this chapter are not meant to be the definitive list of transition items to consider. To build a more extensive checklist, three publications are highly recommended: *Measured Marketing: A Tool to Shape Food Store Strategy,* a research report produced by the Coca-Cola Retailing Research Council (available by calling 800-438-2653), and two reports available from the Publications Department of the Food Marketing Institute (202-452-8444) entitled, *A Guide to Planning Frequent Shopper Programs,* prepared by Willard Bishop Consulting, Ltd. for the Food Marketing Institute, and *Front End Electronic Marketing,* written by Carlene A. Thissen, President, Retail Systems Consulting.

11

Going the distance

Six months after successfully launching your differentiated marketing strategy, 55-65% of all transactions will probably be captured by your card, representing at least 78% of your sales.

By this time, you will have confirmed to your own satisfaction that your customers' ratios and statistics are similar to those of other companies in your particular retail sector. You will have realized that your customer reports demonstrate *clockwork economics* in that the top decile includes the best *recency, frequency*, and *spending* results and, like clockwork, each descending decile's results lessen, as mentioned in Chapter 8.

You will also have discovered that these same clockwork economics apply within a decile. For example, if your top customer decile is broken down into tenths (so that each is now a one-hundredth, or centile, of the original customer database), the same clockwork economics work as you move downwards from the top centile. Each centile has better performance statistics in every category than the centile below! (However, just as clocks don't always keep perfect time, occasionally one decile's or centile's numbers will not follow the perfect symmetrical flow indicated above.)

Best Customer program

Understanding the significance of clockwork economics will lead you to develop a *Best Customer* program. After having studied the information gathered on *your* customers and after gaining insights into their dynamics, you will now have an appreciation of the economic advantages of skewing your reward structure in favor of your best customers.

As explained in earlier chapters, the highest spending customers have a significantly higher gross profit percentage and much greater longevity with you than the lowest spending customers. The top 20% of customers provide over 60% of sales, and the top 30% provide about 75%. Retailers who have developed successful Best Customer programs usually began by focusing on one of these two groups—the top 20 or 30% of their customers. Many refinements followed as additional insights (and confidence!) were gained. Guided by their weekly, monthly, and quarterly customer performance indicators, these retailers kept finding new ways to reward their best customers while lessening the rewards to the other customer segments.

This realignment of rewards and marketing costs continues until incremental profit gains disappear. Then, attention is turned to the next most attractive customer segment. And later the next. This never-ending process is a constant search for optimizing the return on incremental marketing dollars.

Retailers have two primary marketing costs: advertising and markdowns. The Best Customer strategy is based on the premise that matching total marketing costs more closely to sales and customer profitability will increase total profitability. It's simply a matter of prioritizing the allocation of your limited resources.

The Holy Grail of marketing

Over the years most retailers, myself included, have searched for a way to convert our low spending, occasional customers—with their very attractive spending potential—into high spending, frequent customers. This is the Holy Grail of marketing. Unfortunately, no one has yet discovered its secret! Yes, ways have been found to increase these customers' spending and frequency—but the cost of so doing almost always has exceeded the income generated.

It's not a zero sum game

By now, you are probably thinking that if every retailer adopts customer specific marketing, won't we have a zero-sum game with everyone back to where they were before?

In theory, the answer is yes—but only if you and your competitors all move into customer specific marketing at the same time, with identical offers, marketing expenditures and missionary zeal. Of course, this never happens. Some retailing Cyclops will, with great one-eyed intensity, believe he can convert occasional customers into high spending, profitable customers and will devote efforts (and lessening resources) to this quest. Other retailers, imbued with the spirit of King Canute, will believe they can hold back the rising tide of differentiated marketing by continuing their old marketing practices. And still other retailers will instruct middle management to get into customer specific marketing "because everyone else is doing it." In the meantime, the devoted pioneers will be enjoying the superior profit gains which come from their differentiated strategy.

Over time, however, as more and more direct and indirect competitors adopt customer specific marketing as their core strategy, the opportunity for superior gains will probably diminish. But not completely. Because imperfect information will always yield pockets of inefficiency to be exploited, those retailers with an advanced understanding of their customer dynamics will always find new ways to differentiate both their offers and their customers profitably.

Arthur Hughes, a direct marketing expert and author of *Strategic Database Marketing*, believes that some of these superior gains will be permanent. He argues that if customer specific marketing works, it is because it benefits the customers. "It has to be, or it wouldn't work!" he says. "Once you use it to reward your best customers and build a relationship with them, it should increase your profit potential by reducing your marketing costs. In other words, we are shifting from looking at customers as economic machines seeking the lowest price, to looking at them as human beings who want to build a relationship with a supplier that recognizes them and rewards them personally for their behavior. Once you have converted customers to being relationship buyers instead of transaction buyers, your margins should be able to increase. There should be no reason why your increased margin should not continue, even if everyone else is doing it too."

Hitting the sales wall

One major element of differentiated marketing is the rearrangement of our customer mix. Naturally, this rearrangement does have limits, and at some stage, you will hit a sales wall—*the post-rearrangement blues!* What happens is that the sales from your best customers stop compensating for the loss of sales from your least profitable customers (who have stopped shopping with you), even though profits may still be rising.

When you hit this wall, usually a lot of consternation and worrying about what to do next takes place. The first word of advice is not to fall back into your old ways and increase sales for sales sake. Cranking up a series of newspaper advertisements filled with hot specials to attract back the promiscuous shoppers that you have just lost is not logical! Such is but an exercise in profitless prosperity—sales may rise but profits will fall.

Now customer information really starts to help in making more intelligent marketing decisions. You must decide what customer behavior you seek and then find ways to reward that behavior. This is the ideal time for a brainstorming session with your management team to come up with ways to build *profitable* sales. Ideas that may emerge from this session include:

• *Clone Marketing.* Ask an outside data bureau that has comprehensive customer profiles, such as Metromail, to develop an address list of people in your marketing area who are clones of your best customers but who are currently not shopping with you. Then mail a special offer just to them.

• *Partner Programs.* Establish a partners program (if you do not already have one). The potential for new customers being introduced to your stores by partners is significant—and inexpensive!

• *Charitable Programs.* Charitable programs for churches and schools are excellent vehicles for developing new customers. By offering to donate a percentage of the spending of customers associated with these local churches or schools, not only do you enhance the relationship with existing customers linked to those charities, but you also provide a good reason for non-customers to start shopping with you.

• *Refine your product offering.* Invite some of your best customers to special discussion groups, and ask what products they would like to see in your stores that are not currently offered. In this way, you are starting down the road of increasing the share of your customers' total spending. (At the same time, you can eliminate products that your best customers don't purchase.)

• *Refine your offer-bundle.* Re-examine your existing offer-bundle. Think how it could be rearranged to increase sales profitably. For example, how significant are the rewards offered to customers based on their total spending over a three to six-month period? The realignment of your offer-bundle is an ongoing process and, over time, killing even your best programs is wise for two reasons: to avoid an entitlement mentality in customers and to keep your overall offer fresh.

• *Stealth marketing.* Continue to test and measure targeted offers to different customer segments. Experiment with different rewards. For example, what works best for you—offering a *5% off your next purchase* gift certificate or a *$5 off your next purchase* gift certificate? Does this work equally well across all segments, or do some customer segments respond better than others? And how do such offers affect purchase behavior over the next six months?

• *Empowerment.* Encourage your store management teams to learn who their best customers are, and then build relationships with them. In addition, after training them in customer economics, and in how to use their database, seek their help in developing new ways to build profitable sales. Then enlist your department managers in the same quest.

• *Employee rewards.* Introduce store-wide employee rewards based upon both the retention and addition rates of profitable customers.

• *Sub-Clubs.* Negotiate with manufacturers for special offers for selected customer segments, regardless of how much they spend with you. One major retailer already does this, providing an added benefit for cardholders. In 1995, Safeway's mid-Atlantic Division launched its sub-club program in conjunction with the appropriate manufacturers for customer categories such as "Families with Children" and "Health Conscious Households." Each quarter, the households in each sub-club (derived from Safeway's database) receive a package of coupons sponsored by the appropriate manufacturers. PreVision Marketing, Inc. of Lincoln, Massachusetts, runs the program for Safeway. Not only do sub-clubs allow true pinpoint marketing based upon real customer needs, but they also, through the additional benefits provided to specific cardholders, enhance the value of the company's card program. A food retailer has many sub-club opportunities, both large and small—covering areas as diverse as dietetic, pets, wine, small businesses, and restaurants. It's but another illustration of how customer information is changing the face of retailing.

Share groups

One action, that will not only generate many sales-building ideas but will also provide an excellent benchmarking facility, is to start or join a share group devoted exclusively to this subject. Groups I am familiar with have proved extremely valuable to their members. One group, with members from Australia, Europe, and the United States, comes together twice a year just to exchange ideas on their customer specific marketing programs.

Each participant is already a very successful differentiated marketer, yet realizes that much more can be learned in this fast developing field. Because the members don't compete with one another, they are comfortable sharing their confidential results, allowing them to return to their companies with a rich appreciation of what their peers are thinking, doing, and accomplishing. At each meeting, participants relate their latest successes and failures, the experiments they are currently conducting (which are not always glowing successes!), and their results for benchmarking purposes.

If you wish to initiate such a share group, the following agenda may be helpful as you plan your first meeting. Obviously, it should be adapted to suit your group's composition and circumstances.

Initial Meeting Agenda

Part I: Discussion of Participants' Programs

Start with 1-1½ hour presentations by each company.

Possible topics that may be covered include:
1) A brief history of your program.
2) The various elements of your program, such as advertising, customer communications, specials, limits, differentiated offers, and privacy policy.
3) Your competitive situation.
4) Whether you were first, second, etc, into your marketplace with differentiated marketing.
5) Your competitors' reactions—both good and bad, and the reasons.
6) Successes, failures, results, and lessons learned along the way (and any thoughts as to the reasons why).
7) Problems encountered in selling the program internally and how they were overcome.
8) Problems encountered in selling the program externally and how they were overcome (eg, co-op ad allowances, scan-downs, allowances for points).

9) What information you capture and what customer measurements you use.
10) Your key results, including your percentage of cardholder transactions and sales and your defection rates.
11) Experiments you are currently conducting.
12) Areas where you feel your program has gaps.
13) Where you see your program going over the next few years.

Part II: Round Table Discussion

In a round table setting, participants in turn raise a question on which they want general discussion. The following list is typical of the questions that may be raised.

(A) Classifying customers
1) What methods work for you to upgrade *splits* to *loyals*?
2) How might different grades of cards (eg, platinum, gold) work without upsetting other customers?
3) What differentiation programs work for you?
4) What benefits, perceived or real, can be given with a Gold Card to our most loyal customer segment?
5) What is a good cut-off point for Gold status?
6) What about the special case of those senior citizens who are devoted to us, purchase most of their requirements from us, yet do not spend enough for Gold status?
7) How do you practice Customer Management? What are your categories? What do you measure? What are your future plans for customer management?

(B) Building customer loyalty

1) What programs work that strengthen customer loyalty and spending?
2) What are you doing to become closer to customers?
3) How do you *profitably* attract new customers?

(C) Establishing your offer-bundle

1) Which is better—a price- or points-based program?
2) What promotions have worked best for you?
3) What were the results on offers to *loyals, splits, occasionals,* and *newly joined* customers?
4) Have you had any bottom-line success with customer reactivation programs?
5) Under what conditions do you think charging a fee for a membership card would work?

(D) Collecting and measuring information

1) Do any of your statistics significantly differ from any of those presented in the *Measured Marketing* study?
2) How do you use customer information to advantage?
3) What customer information is included in your monthly management reports?
4) How do you incorporate your customer database into customer recovery, customer satisfaction surveys, and product selection/deletion criteria?
5) How does/can customer information redefine the role of store managers?
6) Do you measure either your customers' Life Time Value or their capitalized value? If so, what's your methodology?
7) What customer data do you store? For how long?
8) What customer information do you use on a weekly, monthly, quarterly and annual basis? Why?

(E) Targeting your communications

1) What targeted mailings have you tested? What has worked/not worked for you? How do you use them cost effectively?
2) What newsletters have worked for you? Why?

(F) Handling operational and front-line issues

1) How do you show non-Gold holders that they are not second class citizens?
2) What problems have you had with the privacy issue? How did you handle them?
3) How do you handle a customer who hasn't brought her card to the store yet wants discounts or rewards?
4) How do you discourage customers from applying for a second card if they forget to bring their card?

(G) Handling competitors

1) How do you handle a major competitor launching a card program against you?
2) What refinements do you have up your sleeve, in case of a strong new card-based challenge?
3) Who is your toughest *differentiated* competitor? How are you neutralizing his strengths?
4) How do you compete effectively against competitors' double and triple coupons?

(H) Planning strategically

1) Now that you're ahead, how do you retain your lead? (What new wrinkles can you introduce to differentiate your program further?)
2) Is traditional advertising dead? How much has print advertising decreased since your program launch?

3) After rearranging your customer mix, how do you increase sales profitably, without resorting to more specials, more ads, and more cherry pickers?
4) How do you plan to compete effectively in a future when customers are drowning in cards?
5) How are you changing the battlefield to play to your strengths even further?
6) How are you helping your cardholders by working with manufacturers and vendors?

Part III: Meeting Review

At the end of each meeting, discuss:

1) What are your thoughts on the value of this meeting?
2) Should we plan to meet again?
   a) If so, when and where?
   b) If so, should we invite anyone else to join us?
   c) What should be the invitation criteria?

The questions raised in the above agenda remind us how diverse this subject is and therefore, how slight the possibility of customer specific marketing ever becoming a zero sum game.

All departments are affected

Six months after launch, you will also have realized that customer specific marketing is not just "a marketing thing." It impacts every department. Internally, you may even be considering some reorganization. Externally, relations with your vendors will have altered.

One department that is usually overlooked in this transaction, but is significantly affected, is accounting. The information gathered and reported by this department changes. Budgeting customers slowly begins to take precedence over budgeting sales. Monthly management reports begin incorporating key customer data. Both data capture and information systems start changing to provide direct customer profitability.

Furthermore, to achieve accurate direct profit results by customer, one major traditional buying/accounting practice in food retailing has to change. That is the use of the Suspense (or Promotional) Allowance account. This needs to be replaced with a system of direct product costing. Historically, the Suspense Allowance account has been credited at the end of each quarter (or year) with monies from manufacturers for selling predetermined quantities of their products. In the future, these performance levels will be estimated and incorporated into the ongoing product costs at the time of purchase. Then a quarterly reconciliation will be done to correct any variations, as retailers do today with their percentage rent accounts. This is necessary because the more accurate the customer profitability figures, the better is your decision making.

No turning back

Today, two leading information-based, non-food merchants, Service Merchandise and Radio Shack, know the gross margin by item of every customer purchase. Tomorrow, most food retailers will. Armed with this powerful economic understanding of his customers, a food retailer will have taken giant strides from today's assumption-based marketing practices towards the fact-based marketing of tomorrow.

Further, by drawing on his knowledge of defection rates by customer segment, he will be calculating the capitalized value of his customers and continually making refinements to marketing plans to optimize this value.

Retailers will be like the armies of ages past. Once these armies acquired muskets and cannons, they never reverted to yesterday's weapons—lances, bows and arrows. They poured their efforts into improving their new, technologically advanced weaponry. So, too, will retailers in the decade immediately ahead. Like it or not, all retailers are now on a new battlefield and are in a race for the best, most effective electronic weaponry to win their marketing wars. A new era in retailing has arrived. There is no turning back.

Part VI: Validation

The intention of this final section is to validate what you have been reading.

Chapter 12 shares with you the actual experiences of leading practitioners, expressed from their individual perspectives. It's a fascinating chapter full of insights, practical tips and, most important, reassurance.

Chapter 13 offers a few closing thoughts.

12

In their own words

This chapter comprises speeches by some of the leading practitioners of *customer specific marketing* from around the world. They are included to let you see their perspectives through *their* eyes and to let you see some of the challenges, experiences, and results that they have had. You will gain some extremely valuable insights as you read how each of their companies has applied its unique approach to *customer specific marketing.*

Speeches follow in the following sequence:

Big Y Foods	Dan Lescoe
Gregerson's Foods	Herb Butler
Lees Supermarket	Albert Lees III
Morgan's Tuckerbag	Roger Morgan
Price Chopper	Larry Friedman
Superquinn	Feargal Quinn
Ukrop's Super Markets	Scott Ukrop

Mission Marketing
Presented by
**Daniel J. Lescoe, Vice President of Sales and
Marketing, Big Y Foods, Inc.
Springfield, Massachusetts**
at the Food Marketing Institute's Editors' Briefing,
Chicago, May 2, 1994

Webster defines marketing as an aggregate of functions, involved in moving goods from producer to consumer.

Measured Marketing is collecting, analyzing and using customer information to develop marketing programs.

Then there is *Mission Marketing.* As defined by Big Y Supermarkets, Mission Marketing is an all-out, frontal assault on the competition with our best weapon, the Express Savings Club. Every marketing program we develop has one mission—to promote our Club. It is a religion for us, not just another promotion.

Measured Marketing should not be confused with *Mission Marketing.*

Marketing options

Within our marketing area in 1990, store coupons were the major marketing vehicle used by our competition and by us. Customers in New England loved coupons. At that time, we saw our marketing options as:

A) Stay with our present in-ad coupons and coupon book promotions.
B) Convert to EDLP (every day low pricing).
C) Eliminate coupons and straight-price our programs.
D) Throw away all the traditional marketing methods supermarkets were using and try something new.

We chose "D." We developed what many refer to as a *frequent-shopper card* program, the Express Savings Club.

Our four goals
For our program, we established these goals:
- Offer better service and greater convenience for our customers by eliminating coupons.
- Achieve operational cost savings by improving checkout speed, and eliminating price changes every week.
- Create a progressive image of our company.
- Learn more about our customers to improve our service and value.

> *No more clipping, no more books.*
> *No more cashier's dirty looks!*

Four basic benefits
We established four basic benefits to communicate to our customers:
1) No store coupons to clip.
2) Instant savings on up to five of each item. (Our competitors' coupons limited consumers to savings on one item.)
3) No minimum purchase requirement.
4) Free membership. (A blow to the growing warehouse clubs!)

Also, we visually communicated our new message to the consumer by color-coding all our *electronic* coupons pink (the color of our card) and by placing a "do not clip" border around them. To further emphasize our *clipless coupons*, we designed a sign to use next to each item, the now familiar scissors inside the universal "don't" symbol.

Pre-launch communications

Just prior to launching the program, we mailed a promotional announcement and a new Express Savings Club card to every customer who had a Big Y check cashing card. After the initial mailing, our efforts focused on signing up the universe of customers in our marketing area. We accomplished our goal with total employee commitment and great deals. If you came to shop at Big Y, you didn't leave the store without believing you *needed* an Express Savings Club card. What's more, we made joining easy. A minimum of information was needed and the customer received a temporary membership card immediately. Our customers wanted instant savings, and we gave them instant gratification.

The Club is core

The Express Savings Club was now the core of our marketing efforts. It was clear to our employees, our competition and our customers. Our advertising focused on the benefits of the card; the signs in our stores reinforced the message; our buyers put together great deals to support the program; and our employees asked every customer if they had a card. To say the least, we were deliberate and relentless.

We were so convinced that our mission was right that we even asked our customers to give us their scissors (no need for scissors anymore) and we would give them 10% off their entire grocery bill. But do not try this at home, unless you know where you can safely dispose—environmentally—of hundreds of thousands of scissors!

Making the Club exciting

Our first effort at electronic marketing was tied into Big Y's 55th anniversary. Our scanning computers were programmed to award a free item to every 55th customer using their Express Savings Club. In this case, the free items were from our newly introduced private label line. Other prizes included 55 free trips to destinations all over the world. By the end of our anniversary celebration, our customers were promoting the Club.

Now the challenge was to find new ways to keep the program exciting and add value to the Club. During the first summer, we formed alliances with attractions throughout our marketing area and introduced Sensational Summer. By simply presenting their Express Savings Club card, our customers could save on admission prices to family attractions, such as the Mystic Marinelife Aquarium and the Basketball Hall of Fame. Sensational Summer was a hit! Encouraged by our success, we established ongoing discount agreements for our card members with entertainment and sporting facilities, like our local Civic Center/Symphony Hall complex.

Education Express

Our electronic marketing program broke new ground when we tied our Express card to our new education programs. Big Y has a deep-rooted commitment to education programs. Three years earlier, the company had developed a successful save-a-tape program, Computers for Kids, that donated $1 million to area schools. This time, we decided to use our Express card technology to electronically record purchases and *points* earned for each school.

In January 1992, we launched *Education Express* and *Educating Kids*. Through *Education Express*, Big Y customers could support their local school by simply signing up once for the program and then purchasing money-saving *Education Express* sale items. Every time a participating customer purchased an *Education Express* item, their designated school earned valuable award points electronically! These electronic points were then converted by the schools into free equipment from our Award Catalog. We took the burden of saving, collecting and counting register receipts away. Our Express card made the program easy for our customers and participating schools.

Basically, the program involved these steps:
1) Customers registered for the school of their choice. Each school in our marketing area was assigned a four digit ID number.
2) Our circular advertised *Education Express* sale items using the program's school bus logo.
3) Each *Education Express* sale item had an advertised point value.
4) *Education Express* sale items and point values were identified on the shelf with special *Education Express* signs.
5) Each customer's *Education Express* points were totaled and displayed on their register receipt.
6) Points were electronically tallied for each school and communicated to them on a bi-weekly basis.
7) Schools order from our Award Catalog.

No more tapes to save! Over 750 schools and 68% of our weekly customer base actively participated in the program, earning close to $2 million for computers, science equipment, musical instruments, and much more.

Educating Kids

Our second education initiative was a 36-page magazine, *Educating Kids*. Articles in the magazine were geared to parents of school-aged children and offered practical tips, advice, and guidance for parental involvement in education. With 400,000 free issues published quarterly, the publication represented the largest campaign for parental involvement in education in the United States. The magazine also served as a vehicle to promote *Education Express*: each issue featured over 200 *Education Express* sale items.

Education Express and *Educating Kids* have been our two most rewarding programs. We helped make a difference in education and added a real value to our card.

Express Millions

This past February, we unveiled our latest card-based program, *Express Millions*. By simply having their card scanned in our store, customers can win $1 instant lottery tickets, $50 free groceries or $1,000 cash instantly. All $1,000 winners are automatically entered into two sweepstakes drawings for a chance to win vacations, cars, and the grand prize of $1 million.

Electronic Triple Coupons

Recently, we introduced "electronic" triple coupons. Big Y, like our competition, automatically doubles the value of manufacturer coupons. Periodically, a competitor would advertise three triple coupons for the week. Naturally, the customer had to clip the coupons. Then, one competitor offered to match triple coupons from other retailers. Big Y answered by telling our customers we would redeem their three highest valued manufacturers' coupons *electronically.* No need to clip the competitors' triples. What's more, they couldn't bring our electronic triples to a competitor's store.

How are we doing?

We're often asked to quantify the success of our Express Savings Club. Due to the highly competitive nature of our business, our statistical information, like our customer database, is kept confidential. I believe, however, that a comparison of our 1990 vs. 1993 sales and market share in western Massachusetts tells the whole story. In 1990 Big Y sales in the four counties of western Massachusetts were $272,400,000, which represented 25.37% of the market. In 1993, we moved into the number one position with sales of almost $364,662,474 and a market share of 28.75%. During this same period, market share for each of our two primary competitors fell more than 4%.

Total commitment

In closing, *Mission Marketing* requires total commitment. At Big Y, all marketing decisions are based onwhether they fit with our Express Savings Club. Every new program must improve and advance our card. *Mission Marketing* is not for the meek or faint at heart.

Frequent-shopper Programs: Four Questions
Presented by
**Herb Butler, Manager of Information Services,
Gregerson's Foods Inc. Gadsden, Alabama**
at the Food Marketing Institute's Marketechnics
Conference, Houston, February 20, 1995

It's my pleasure to be here with you today to discuss some of the processes involved in planning a frequent-shopper program. In the next few minutes, I want to concentrate on four key program planning areas. I will raise questions about those areas and give you, I hope, practical answers that will aid you in your quest for knowledge regarding frequent-shopper and electronic marketing programs.

Let me begin with a brief look at my company. Gregerson Foods operates ten stores in northeastern Alabama and northwestern Georgia. We have six conventional Gregerson Super Markets and four limited assortment stores. Of our six supermarkets, five range in size from 28,000 to 35,000 square feet, and our flagship store, which you see here on this slide, located in Gadsden, Alabama, is 72,000 square feet. All six are within a 40-mile radius of Gadsden, in a tri-county region of about 250,000 people.

In April of last year, we kicked off our *Club Greg* program in our six super markets. DCI was our card marketing partner. We have issued 90,000 cards in ten months. And we now have 62,000 households in our market area with a Club Greg card.

The four questions

Today, I will answer four practical questions in the area of program planning:
1) *Training.* How much is enough?

2) *Program pricing.* How do we maximize the impact?
3) *Long term hook.* What is it, and how do we do it?
4) *Advertising.* How do we make the transition into marketing?

1) Training

Our first question concerns *training*. How much is enough? It's important to remember that customers learn the program from our associates which makes training a vital part of the success of a program. The entire program is a team effort that begins at the top, including training. And the bottom line here is that training is a continuous process. You can never over-do training. With Club Greg training, we had all associates attend information meetings. Over 95% of our associates attended these meetings. We discussed the program in detail, but we also gave our associates some background information about the concept of electronic marketing as a whole. As I indicated, upper management involvement is essential—these store meetings were conducted by the President, the COO and myself, as the program director. Advanced training was given to all of our sign-up personnel and our customer service personnel. We also have follow-up training for all front-end personnel about every six months.

2) Pricing

The second area of program planning for us to examine is *program pricing* and how you maximize its impact. There are two thoughts in this area. The first is to have a few discounts with big savings, and the second is to have many discounts with moderate savings. Of course, the bottom line here is that you really can never have too many deals.

With Club Greg's deals and discounts we have incorporated both ideas into our pricing plan. We have 10-20 items in our weekly ad with significant discounts, and we have 600-900 Temporary Price Reductions, or TPR's, around the store, with moderate discounts. To gain any of these discounts, a customer must present his or her Club Greg card at the checkout.

This move was a major point of concern in our company. However, we found that putting all of our TPR's on the program did not turn out to be a significant problem. In fact, customers like it because they see more savings on their register receipts.

We also have everyday discounts and deals in high gross, but low volume, departments. For example, if a customer uses her *Club Greg* card when she buys a greeting card, she receives a free postage stamp at the check-out; a dollar is taken off all fresh-baked cakes in our bakery when she uses the card; and if a customer uses her card when she buys a deli pizza, she gets $0.50 off that!

3) Long term hook

Let's now take a look at the third point, the *long term hook*. What does that mean and how do we do it? Of course, the phrase *short-term look and long-term hook* was made popular by Brian Woolf in his *Measured Marketing Report* conducted for the Coca-Cola Retailing Research Council and released last year. What it means is that you give the customer a short-term look to get them interested, but then a long-term hook is required to keep them returning (and presenting their card). Value is critical, while different, for both.

Take a quick look at our short-term look with Club Greg. Basically it's what I've just described. We have cardholder discounts in our weekly ads and our TPR's, and we also provide them check-cashing privileges, which is a very important part of the program.

Our long-term hook with Club Greg is our points-based reward system which gives our customers one point for every dollar they spend. Rewards are then given as they achieve different thresholds. We've had exciting give-aways and sweepstakes. For example, Brian Woolf, in the previous workshop this morning, described some things that you can do creatively with turkeys at Thanksgiving. At Thanksgiving last year, we gave 12,000 turkeys free to our customers as a way of saying "Happy Holidays." It worked very well! Also, we have had some exciting tie-ins with the local media. For example, last Fall we gave away a truck in a promotion called "Trucking with Club Greg." We did that with a local radio station and it created a lot of excitement. Our program theme really sums up the theory behind the long-term hook by declaring that *loyalty pays rewards*. We have this theme on all of our mailings and on a lot of our store signage.

4) Advertising

The last question regarding program planning concerns *advertising*. How do we move to marketing? There's an old saying that half of all advertising dollars are wasted. The only problem is trying to find out which half! Well, transforming your ad budget and making a transition into marketing is a key part of a frequent-shopper program. At Gregerson's, we discontinued all promotions several months before start-up—and we had been running quite a bit! We were trying to be everything to everybody. For example, we had a senior citizens discount program as well as offering double coupons; and we discontinued both about three months before the launch of our Club Greg program, so we took quite a hit!

We strategically placed teaser spots on radio and TV to let our customers know what was coming, but we didn't get too specific on that. And then we ran an informational newspaper ad the day of implementation, explaining the plan in more detail. Finally, we made a weekly transition in our weekly newspaper ad. We started out with four items the first week, and have moved up to twelve, and sometimes as many as twenty-five items in our ad. And usually 85 to 90% of the items in our ad will be Club Greg specials only.

We have been able to significantly cut back our advertising budget. Our biggest cost—newspaper advertising—we've been able to cut 55%. We went from running two double truck ads every week to just a single page once a week.

We had already cut back radio and television advertising significantly in the three-month lull before we launched Club Greg. We have since cut back radio advertising a further 25% and television advertising an additional third. What we've done is taken those savings and used them for direct marketing and target marketing. And we are just about to install some more tracking software, which will allow us to take a closer look at our promotional sales and redemptions, so that we can better target our advertising dollars.

Video, radio and TV

To give you some specific examples of what we did with our advertising, I have a short video clip with both our radio and TV spots that we ran at the beginning of the program. Let's take a look at them...

"Just ten days until Club Greg. The most exciting revolution to take place in grocery shopping ever! The new Club Greg card will make shopping fun—really fun! It will save you money and will do many more exciting fun things for you, too. But we only have a few seconds left to tell you that *the more you use the Club Greg card, the more you save!* Just ten days until grocery shopping will be changed forever! And it's exclusively from Gregerson's Foods!"

"You've been hearing about it, and it's finally here! It's Club Greg, and it's exclusively at Gregerson's Foods. What is Club Greg? It's a buying service, and membership is free! All you have to do is drop by any Gregerson's location and sign up. As a Club Greg member, you'll be entitled to extra discounts on hundreds of items, check cashing privileges, even a chance to win wonderful prizes and much, much more! Get your Club Greg card today at any location of Gregerson's. Club Greg—it's your passport to savings, service, and smiles, exclusively from Gregerson's."

"Psst! Want to save a bundle on your grocery bill? You can, starting April 6th. It's Club Greg from Gregerson's. And it's free! I can't tell you everything, but I can tell you the more you use it, the more you save! Club Greg. Only at Gregerson's."

"At Gregerson's, we are always looking for ways to save you money on your food bill. But this is the most exciting thing we've ever done! It's the Club Greg card. It's free and it can save you money every time you use it. This card gives you great new ways to save. Extra discounts on hundreds of items, check cashing privileges, and the chance to win lots of fabulous prizes! Club Greg: it's your passport to savings, service and smiles, and it's only from Gregerson's."

Planning is important

Training, pricing, the *long-term hook* and *advertising* are all important factors to consider when planning your frequent-shopper program.

I've enjoyed the opportunity to share my company's experiences with you, and if you are planning to launch a frequent-shopper program, I hope that you experience minimum pain and maximum gain!

The Case Against Conventional Advertising
Presented by
**Albert Lees III, President, Lees Supermarket,
Westport, Massachusetts**
at the Food Marketing Ideas Exchange Group
Grand Rapids, Michigan, September 14, 1995

Lees Supermarket, like most companies in this room, has been wrestling with the entire concept of the cost effectiveness of advertising. The classic arguments have always been:

- How do we attract new customers if we don't advertise?

- I have to stay with my competition, and they advertise every week in the local newspaper!

- What will happen to sales if we stop advertising?

- Volume drives the business, and we only get volume from advertising.

We have spent almost one entire year analyzing and using information collected in our database system. While we admittedly have a long, long way to go with this whole concept, the information that we have gathered is applicable to all of us, not just those companies in a card-based marketing program. All that the card allows us to do, in this instance anyway, is collect the relevant information and analyze it to decide future strategies. And, guess what?—Our company's findings are not substantially different from other companies around the world! Chances are these findings are not substantially different from your own!

I want to share the preliminary findings of how our customers and shoppers act and react at Lees Supermarket, with and without advertising, and then share with you some of our thoughts and ideas that we will be trying out in the next six months.

Our Advertising Since January 1, 1995

We had decided in late 1994 to try eliminating our conventional advertising format (an eight-page, two-week flyer mailed to every household in our trade area) and experiment with other forms of promotion. The reasons were our gut feeling that we were wasting our advertising money and Brian Woolf's prodding that conventional forms of advertising only work to reward the cherry picker, but really do nothing for the real measures of business success—loyal customers and profitability. So we decided to give it a try.

During the first five weeks of January, we replaced our conventional item/price mass-mailed flyer with:

1) A *Reward Yourself* promotional program that allowed people to qualify for any one of four amounts of *percentage-off* discount certificates;
2) An in-store *hot sheet* with very hot specials in all departments; and
3) Spot newspaper advertising reminding customers of our in-store promotion.

Results for the five-week promotion were a 6.2% increase in sales compared with the same five weeks of 1994 and a 15% increase in profitability compared to the same period last year.

We continued to advertise on an in-store basis only until our Grand Re-Opening beginning June 19, 1995. While it was planned that we would make a big splash with our advertising for this period, we were also looking forward to going back to a more conventional format, as our sales had been increasing at only a 3-4% rate for the first six months of 1995—although our profits were substantially higher! Any correlation?

During the summer of 1995, we continued to advertise to every household in our trade area, first on an every-week basis (for approximately six weeks), and then on our regular two-week basis. (This is ongoing.) Further, we dropped *all perishables* from our ad in early August, choosing to go with an in-store *hot sheet* for all perishable items. The results? We posted consistent 10-15% increases in business throughout the entire summer! Any change in the advertising format brought no change whatsoever in our sales volume. And our profitability kept pace with the increases in business! But I attribute this increase in business to:

• *An addition of 8,000 square feet of sales area* which allowed us to create a selection and assortment of food unlike any other store in our area. (Our sales per transaction increased 10-12%.)

• *The weather.* It was almost too good to be true— almost no rain at all. Generally excellent business conditions for everyone on the East Coast. From North Carolina to Maine, record sales and profits were reported.

Needless to say, we spent many days scratching our heads, trying to figure this whole thing out. And although we continue to resist the conclusion, there is really no doubt in my mind that conventional forms of advertising, done on a consistent basis, do nothing for the long-term viability of our business!

In other words, I believe that we are wasting tens of thousands of dollars, directed at something that does nothing to increase or enhance our long-term business.

So, if I think that advertising isn't working, then what's going on with our customers? The following observations are what we have found about our customer base. They give a lot of insight into what is, and what isn't, happening!

Observation #1 ... 1% per week

You will, almost by default, attract new customers to your stores at the rate of approximately 1% of your entire customer base every week, with or without advertising!

This is a Brian Woolf *truism* which needs to be seen to be believed. During the thirteen weeks from March 6 through May 29, we averaged 121 new card members a week. However, if you factor out weeks 12 and 13—Memorial Week—the traditional start of our summer season, we averaged 103 new members per week. Our card base during that time increased from 8,276 to 9,853—so that 103 average is mighty close to that 1% figure. This happened during a 5Ω month period when we were doing *no* external advertising at all! In short, these people walked in off the street, for reasons other than the traditional forms of advertising.

Observation #2 ... new customer frequency

Measuring new customer frequency, we found that as few as 50% and as many as 71% of all new customers shopped with us six times or less! And this occurred over a period as long as 26 weeks!

Remember that this was, and continues to be, the activity of people who come into our store for whatever reason...word of mouth, curiosity, convenience, new in town, and so on.

This behavior was almost identical when we began mailing our flyers again to kick off our Grand Re-Opening. During that week, when we decided to let the world know that we were having a Grand Re-Opening of our new addition and remodeled store, 364 new customers signed up for a Lees Shoppers Club Card. Over the next ten weeks, 68% shopped with us fewer than six visits and 48.63% shopped with us between one and three times!

Observation #3 ... new customer markdowns

Fifty percent of the total number of new customers from our Grand Opening Week shopped with us one to three times. However, their markdowns were 15%—twice the amount of the next group (four to six visits) and 3.75 times the over twenty visit group!

In essence, what we did was to spend a lot of money on advertising to customers who came in, cherry-picked us of our specials, and then left! Interestingly enough, this is the behavior and the statistics of the new customers from March 6, 1995, through May 29, 1995—when we were not advertising at all. So we had no different reaction from our new customers during the Grand Opening Week, just more of them!

Observation #4 ... customer profitability

We have calculated that the approximate going-in-gross for Lees Supermarket is 35% before all specials and shrink. At this time of year, our operating expenses are approximately 22.75% of sales. If this one to three visit group hit us for 15% in markdowns, it would appear that we had a coming-out gross profit for this group of 20% or 2.75% less than we need to cover our operating expenses!

Now, this is not totally true because we all know that there are fixed costs and variable costs with any business. However, using the figures provided on our decile chart, it is clear that our top three deciles contribute 100% to the total cost of operating this business. In theory, if you lost the bottom 70% of your entire customer base, you would still break even and pay yourself a living wage!

Observation #5 ... it all happens in the top half

During a four-week test in the middle of summer of

our core marketing area (all 636 and 635 telephone area codes), we found out the following about customers in our core territory:

1) The top decile contributed 47.45% of the net profit of our core customers; while the next four deciles combined contributed 50.4%, for a total of 97.85%. The bottom five deciles contributed virtually nothing to the bottom line of Lees Supermarket!

2) Twenty-five percent of all markdowns within this core group were taken by the bottom five deciles, although they only account for 15% of the sales volume, and zero profit.

3) Remember that when we speak of deciles, we are dividing up the customer base into ten equal segments, so the number of customers in the bottom five deciles is the same as in the top five deciles.

4) The bottom five deciles shopped us a shade better than once every two weeks, while the top five deciles shop 1.67 times per week. Greater frequency equates to greater sales through greater exposure to products and services. It also shows a greater commitment to the relationship of customer and retailer.

Conclusions

1) Advertising in a conventional format does not appear to have any significant value to the operation of the business.

2) The people who we consider customers are coming into our store on a regular basis anyway, and they are not motivated to shop with us based upon what's on special that particular week.

3) New customers show up on a regular weekly basis—whether we advertise or not.

4) Not advertising perishables in our flyer had no negative impact on our overall sales. For example, we had smoked shoulders on sale last week, for $0.48 per pound,

limit one per family per week. This was an in-store special only. We sold out of fifty cases of the product by Saturday afternoon and could have sold another fifteen. We sold as many smoked shoulders this week as we did the last time when it was advertised to 12,000 households. The price that time was higher, $0.68 per pound, but there was no limit. And our gross profit dollars have been consistently higher.

5) We have not advertised produce items in the flyer for over two years, but our produce business grows 20-25% every single year! And the in-store sale items still sell like crazy!

6) We are still not doing enough for our best customers, although additional markdowns do not seem to turn on this loyal group.

7) From other data, there is a wide variation even within deciles on the amount of money spent on food dollars at Lees Supermarket. There are more food dollars to be gotten even out of our best customers. The question is how?

8) Redirecting advertising and markdown dollars to the deciles that will give us the most bang for the buck seems to be more preferential than giving it across the board and having the lower deciles take money from the upper deciles. This Robin Hood mentality can only stop if you think like the Sheriff of Nottingham! Remember though, that like the tale itself, the lower classes were turned on more by money than the upper classes, who were turned on more by power, privilege, and protection of their stature in the kingdom. We must strike a balance between pampering our best customers and not causing a revolution at the bottom, because that revolution may destroy the kingdom!

Measuring & Maximizing Customer Retention
Presented by
**Roger Morgan, Managing Director, Morgan's
Tuckerbag Supermarkets, Melton, Vic., Australia**
at the Relationship Marketing Conference, Golden
Gate Hotel, Sydney, Australia, February 20, 1995

This presentation is from a business that up to recently had completed over twenty-one years of traditional supermarket retailing. Over the last two years this operation has had its whole methodology of operation *re-engineered* so it is able to deliver numerous *points of difference* to its customers.

To take on this task, *all of us in the business had to change a lifetime of mindsets* developed over the many years of our working lives, and as a business, we had to break down many paradigms. Many of our people were unable to deal with it, and had to move on during the transition while others simply blossomed.

We did experience a major paradigm shift.

One of those primary points of difference, and I emphasize *one of the primary points,* was the introduction of a frequency marketing program.

Business background

Before I go any further, let me give you a thumbnail sketch of the business I am about to talk about. The Morgan family (my brothers Peter and Neal and myself, with our parents) own and operate four Tuckerbag Supermarkets and two Payless Superbarns in the towns of Melton, Bacchus Marsh, Sunbury and Werribee in Melbourne's western region.

Our Tuckerbag Supermarkets project an upmarket, people-oriented, high service philosophy. Our Payless

Superbarns, which are in direct competition to our Tuckerbags, as well as significant representatives of our national chains, while most certainly people oriented, are limited in their services but cheap in their retail pricing. The supermarkets within the Morgan group offer a full range of groceries and liquor, supported by an extensive offer of fresh produce, delicatessen, meat and bakery.

The birth of our frequent shopper program

Early in May 1992, after a lot of lobbying by ourselves and some of our peers, we were able to generate some interest from our supplier of software in the writing of a frequent-shopper program that could easily be operated in our type of retail environment.

Loyalty Manager and *Reward Manager* were the result of this activity, and both directly interface into the ICL 9518 front-end terminals.

Loyalty Manager is the component that maintains the customer database, the frequency marketing attributes and historical activity files, while *Reward Manager* provides instant gratification or, in real terms, *electronic coupons*, that give an instant reward to club members on a pre-determined range of products.

Morgan's piloted both of these programs at their Melton Tuckerbag site in March 1993, quickly followed at our Sunbury Tuckerbag in May, and then at Bacchus Marsh Tuckerbag in June of the same year.

The registered name of our frequency marketing program is *Extra Shopping Power* or ESP, and using a play on words we hand-picked our most jovial and outgoing team members, dressed them up as wizards, and with a lot of "theatre," set out to sign up every customer who walked in the door, and achieved that aim as each store was brought on line.

Low margins, low cost

The nature of our business with its particularly low margins demanded that we implement any program such as this at the lowest cost possible. Certainly, smart cards and magnetic stripe cards were investigated and proved not a consideration due to cost; so with scanners on every supermarket checkout lane, for us, bar-coding was the obvious method.

Our application form is a one-third preprinted A4 with two key tags pre-perforated which we bar-code ourselves utilizing existing printers and software. The key tags are provided to our customers with the same plastic carriers that are commonly supplied by the RACV. These can be purchased in bulk for around $0.06 each. The total setup costs about $0.20, plus labor, per customer.

Our offer components

Our offer consists of the following components:

1) An Instant Reward on a variable number of items that are locked in for variable periods and, in real terms, now replace many of the open reductions we had in the past.

These are advertised at the point of sale—be it the shelf or off-location display showing both the normal price and the club members' price, clearly identifying the incentive to become a member of the club. Items offered are mostly grocery. However, a substantial range of liquor, fruit and vegetables, and meat are also offered.

This fulfills the instant gratification desires of our customers, and we ensure that they are aware of their savings by printing the amount saved against each line item and the total saved on the bottom of each register docket.

Clearly, this illustrates to our customers the financial benefits of belonging to the club at the point of payment and tends to become a subject of pride for them because they are able now to rationalize much of their spending by their volume of identifiable and measurable savings. The receipt, among other things, displays the line item ESP savings, the total ESP savings, and the customer's ESP points balance at the end of the prior day.

2) A quality Gift Shop Showcase is on show in each store, and it overflows with an extensive range of wanted items that would normally retail between $5.00 and $250.00 that can be purchased with ESP vouchers issued on the basis of one dollar spent earns one point.

Some examples of the many selections are:
19,500 points - Johnnie Walker Blue Label Scotch
5,000 points - Ronson Milk Shake Maker
4,000 points - Crystal wine goblets, set of 4
3,000 points - Matching crystal wine decanter
1,500 points - Silver-plated placemats, set of 2
1,000 points - Six matching silver-plated coasters
500 points - Silver-plated napkin holder.

Each item in each showcase carries an adhesive label that identifies its stock number, item description and the number of points required to purchase it. We created this customer information item from that module within our scan support system which prints the shelf labels for all of our stores.

All of these items are fully maintained in our master scan file and are scan-sold like any other item at the checkout, except that they are paid for with vouchers instead of cash. Furthermore, full Inventory Management is employed through our D.S.D. system to ensure that perfect stock control disciplines are maintained.

This illuminated high profile glass and chrome show-case is displayed in such a way that it is seen by all who enter the store before they commence shopping. This triggers the desire to achieve the number of points need-ed and stimulates the requirement to buy.

As soon as each customer's account exceeds 250 points, our system automatically advises our cashier when the customer's ESP card is scanned. A blank voucher is then inserted for validation and handed to the customer. Once the validation process is actioned, the 250 ESP points are automatically subtracted from that customer's file.

These ESP vouchers are saved by our customers until they have enough to purchase their chosen item. Clearly our best and most loyal customers earn the biggest rewards, and they earn them most frequently.

This fulfills our desire to generate a reason for our customers to bypass all of the other supermarkets, butchers, delicatessens, fruiterers, bakeries, liquor retailers, tobacconists, and so on. Our objective is for our customers to purchase every need (that we are able to supply) from us and no one else.

3) A free Key Finder Service. Our key tag suggests that a potential finder of lost keys drop them in a mail box, and as a service we will return them to their owner. This assists us in selling the objective of having our card on every customer's key ring. I find it personally very satis-fying to have the opportunity to phone one of our customers and tell her that we have found the keys that she had lost. This always results in gaining another cus-tomer "for life."

4) A free Christmas Club where our customers deposit a few dollars each week (often their change) into their account that is linked to their ESP card. This is a very quick and effective task at the cashiers' keyboard as it is only one extra keystroke in the transaction. During the first week in December, we post a voucher to the value of their deposit to each customer. Vouchers are only redeemable in our stores.

5) *Tuckers Cubby Club* is a children's birthday club, where our Tuckerbag character logo *Tucker* sends birthday greetings plus vouchers for free popcorn, puppets, pencils, erasers, rulers, etc. which the child tenders at the store to collect his/her gifts. ESP in this instance stands for Extra Special People.

We also enclose a slip offering personalized cartoon-topped birthday cakes (at an excellent gross profit) from our bakery, plus vouchers for free or discounted items from other local non-competing appropriate businesses. Recently we added a Children's Party Pack offer to the mailer that provides the basics for an eight-children celebration for under $40.00, and they are selling extremely well.

Other business houses help us deliver an agreed benefit to the children of our customers, and in real terms this part of the operation can become self-funding as we charge for each insertion.

6) *A Community Assistance program* was also spawned by ESP, where local clubs, churches, schools, sporting associations and the like are able to receive one percent of all of the purchases, within a pre-determined two-month period, of any of their members or supporters that they sign up into ESP.

We pay this every two months in the form of a voucher redeemable in our stores, and it is accompanied by a listing of the name of all of the supporters that they have signed up with the value of their component of the donation, and it is sorted in order of highest to lowest.

This has permitted us to withdraw from the rat race of trying to be a good local business citizen to everyone—at a terrible cost with little return—and has dispensed with the extreme cost and frustration of trying to assist with every request. All donations are now channeled through this facility, and we are now achieving a lot of added value for the funds we put back into the community.

Once again our best supporters receive the biggest rewards and the voucher returns them to our store. These Community Service donations are funded by cutting back part of our mass media expenditure.

Our database

We currently have 40,000 households on our database and an incredible and extensive knowledge of shopping habits of those households.

As well as collecting the cardholder's name and address details on the application form, we request the following:

- Christian name of spouse.
- Wedding Anniversary.
- Names and birth dates of children under ten years.
- Each time the card is scanned, the system collects and records the following primary data:
  ◊ The total dollars spent this week, this month, and every month for the past twelve months.
  ◊ A breakup of the dollars spent in each of our ten primary departments.
  ◊ Dollars spent on items at normal price.
  ◊ Dollars spent on items at a reduced or special price.
  ◊ Every individual purchase during the current month, which store it occurred in, the date of the transaction, the operator that processed it, and the time of day.
  ◊ Year-to-date total of each member's Instant Reward savings.

Our systems run on a personal computer at store level in a slave format which simply collects all of the data during trading hours, then dials into our Support Center during the night, and transfers the information on to our master system that resides on a two-gigabyte Unix platform. All of our management activity occurs at our Support Centre. However, the software can stand alone in a single site on DOS, if required that way.

Direct customer communications

Included within the software is a word processor and mail merge interface. This permits numerous letters for all types of occasions to be created and maintained on file for re-use as required. These can be merged with the customer database utilizing whatever parameters are requested to target a particular audience.

Examples of letters are:

- A simple no strings *Thanks for shopping with us* to our best, most loyal customers.

- To customers who have not shopped for the last six weeks.

- To customers who shop regularly, but do not shop a particular department.

- A welcome to our new ESP members.

- Advice to our customers regarding their Instant Reward savings over a given period.

Where we believe we have a problem, we include an offer to entice our customer to try us again or try that specific department that they do not use. This could be in the form of a voucher or a series of vouchers that are simply too good not to use.

This, of course, has grown into a fairly significant in-house direct mail operation. We handle the physical side of folding and insertion by utilizing a local Welfare

Agency that sources suitable work for disabled people, which works very well for both parties.

Customer segmentation

We have identified that our business clearly has "gold" and "copper" types of customers, plus a range in between, and we have clearly satisfied ourselves that not all of our customers are equal. This was real earth-shattering stuff!

Database customer category segmentation is exciting when you have clean concise current data which is updating daily, and this is where the real firepower is. We are only now starting to reap the benefits of months of intense activity in this field.

Our initial results tell us that a typical supermarket could have a customer base, of whom on average at the top end, less than 20% would be termed very loyal, while at the bottom end there is another 20%, who spend only about $9.00 per week, with 35% of that in specials. Imagine, $9.00 per week and $3.25 of that is at promotional prices! What do we do? We give those cherry pickers who, in real terms, cost us money, a priority "eight items or less" fast lane! *Our industry has definitely got it all wrong!*

The middle 60% we call *splits*, and these are those who visit us regularly but based on their spend rate, they are clearly what we would probably term *promiscuous shoppers*, because they hang around other stores as well as ours. These are the ones we focus on in an effort to upgrade them to *loyals*.

Does It Work?—Yes!

In an industry that has seen average customer transaction values dropping, and customer visits increasing, our stores with this program in place radically went against this trend. We experienced increased (and still increasing!) customer transaction values with increased customer traffic as well! Some identical weeks, this year versus last year, have experienced over 40% sales increases, with year-to-date increases in the 20% plus range above the comparable period last year. The best news, however, is a better bottom line—a very much better bottom line!

What Does It Cost?

In our environment, in real terms, nothing! We are redirecting our local advertising budget into this form of marketing and have dispensed with the insane repetition of weekly supermarket handbills (circulars) that all of us in this industry use to clutter the mailboxes of our—and everyone else's—customers, each and every weekend.

A classic example of this insanity is the fact that we have been distributing 10,000 Tuckerbag handbills per week in one town for years. Yet in this town we have only signed up 5,000 households in ESP (99% of our regular customers). Therefore half of our printing and distribution costs for years has really been useless in converting customers, as well as an incredible waste of money.

Somebody once said, "Only half of your advertising works. Unfortunately we never knew which half." But now we do!

Our up-front costs were minimal due to the relationship we had built with our supplier of both hardware and software and some longer-term planning that paid off. The hardware component was already in place. All we had to do was load the software to make this most valuable asset work harder.

Our ongoing intention is to mainstream this activity and as a result, we have shifted our local press and handbill budgets to this new form of marketing.

What Is The Future?

We have not even scratched the surface yet! Something new comes up every week. There's always another angle!

One of our most successful ideas has been to identify the *five highest customer sales each day*. We print out their data profile and then phone them. They are asked how they enjoyed their shopping experience yesterday, and was there anything that they could not find or were there any problems, etc. We seek information about any departments that they do not shop, to allow us to, later on, target an offer to have them try that department again. On completion of this phone call of recognition we flag that file not to re-appear *on this cycle*, to permit us, over a period of time, to talk to all of our customers from the biggest purchaser down.

Another idea is that when we receive a complaint, it is obviously handled to our best ability, but often we are unsure of how effective *our complaint management skills* are. We are able to measure how effective we have been by recoding that particular customer's activity data at that point and then comparing it over the following weeks and months. By monitoring their activity, we are able to re-visit this customer should their purchasing not be up to the levels that it once was.

We are able to *identify those who do not shop any particular department* and entice them to lift their expenditure during their following visits by posting a specific coupon or series of coupons.

As a result of customer focus groups suggesting that they couldn't achieve the necessary points for their chosen Gift Shop Showcase selections quickly enough, we invited *non-competing local business houses* to participate in our Extra Sales Potential offer. We sell them sheets of 100 point ESP adhesive stamps at a discounted rate that will cover the purchase of gifts, advertising material and stationery. These businesses then offer them as an incentive to purchase from them in preference to their competitors. Our ESP logo is now displayed in over fifty other shop windows in our towns, and the number of participants is growing.

Once we are satisfied that we are maximizing the purchasing potential of our existing customers, we will then, and only then, seek new ones. This will be actioned by first *identifying every potential customer* in a pre-defined primary area via the electronic Electoral Roll or telephone book. This database will then be run against our own, and all those not listed will be targeted with an offer they cannot refuse. These will be distributed in small manageable quantities, so that when they come into the store and identify themselves as this specific coupon holder, we will have our team members ready to unleash the greatest P.R. job they have ever struck.

We term this activity, in particular, *Stealth Marketing*. However, all of this really comes under that title. This form of customer creation will be as efficient, as effective, and as precise as one of these modern war machines that we saw deliver warheads into those ventilation ducts during the Gulf War.

The Incredibly Important Service Component

Once we have those people in store, then we unleash the most important support component to any Loyalty Management program and that is our "Positively Outrageous Customer Service That Will Knock Their Socks Off!"

Points of Difference

I spoke of Points of Difference earlier ...
*   A 1-800 Hot Line customer phone number to the owners of our business;

- A supply of Freepost return Customer Suggestion Slips;
- A supermarket that writes its customers simply to thank them for being regular shoppers;
- Regular customer focus group meetings;
- Identification of *each* ESP member's name electronically at the checkout, but only to the cashier so that she is able to greet and thank her by name without the customer being aware of the prompt;
- Our own developing range of "Killer" brand, fresh products not available anywhere else: "Killerburgers®," "Killerpizzas®," Killerdonuts®." Sound "korny" to you?

These are examples that we deliver daily to support our customer retention program.

New competitive openings

What happens when a new supermarket opens in one of our towns? We know the name and address of every single customer of ours who has strayed, and we will know immediately. Obviously, they will be targeted with a series of offers that they will find absolutely impossible to refuse.

Effective Training

A dedication to intensive training is, without any doubt, the insurance policy to ensure that all of the expense, resources, and time that go into the launching of this type of program maximize the required effect on customers.

Without the basic knowledge throughout all levels of the team, including those who do not have much direct contact with customers, the weapon begins to be diluted very quickly.

Prior to each launch, our Team Development Manager spent as much time as was necessary, with groups of eight to ten people, to introduce every member to the program principles and to explain *how* and, most important, *why* we are doing this. I emphasize that absolutely every member participated.

Most of these people were not instructed in the mechanics, but in the selling skills and logic, so that they could put forward a positive, knowledgeable answer to any questions raised by our customers. A sense of ownership by everyone was achieved from Butchers, Goods Receivers, Shelf Fillers, Bakers—the whole team.

Team Discount

To further cement team support, we dispensed with the 5% employee discount that we had delivered for years, and now supply our team with double points each time they purchase with the card. This clearly is a winner with the team and removes humans from the whole operation, as the system knows they are employees and automatically awards the double points. Now our people, because they are experienced at receiving points, are so much better as our selling agents.

Mission statement

Our mission statement is very simple—*To have happy customers.*

This program has been instrumental in our endeavours to deliver the primary objective for that Mission.

Four closing thoughts

1) A few words of caution. This type of program is *not a panacea for ailing sales;* it is but one—albeit a major— component in the whole retail armory of options.

Furthermore, this type of program, in my opinion, will make a good business better, while it will probably be instrumental in destroying an already poor business.

2) As the twenty-first century approaches, I believe independent retailers need to employ guerrilla tactics to protect what is left of their diminishing market share, particularly as most of us do not have the funding resources to mount a major offensive against the corporate giants. It is painfully clear that we are unable to fight the Goliaths on their turf using their rules—we survivors must develop our own form of guerrilla warfare.

3) I am convinced that *positively outrageous customer service,* coupled with a dose of basic marketing talent, a desire to utilize technology and be unafraid to look change in the face—and slap it—can be the weapon to neutralize the big guys.

4) It is great to go to work every day with the knowledge that the big guys really haven't got a "smick" about what on earth we are up to with ESP this week!!!!

Remember the Mustard!
Presented by
**Larry Friedman, Vice President Financial Services,
Price Chopper Inc., Schenectady, New York**
at the MasterCard Conference, Chicago, June 8, 1995

We got into electronic marketing when it was just a vision—actually back in 1987. So I'm going to take you through the evolution in history. Why did we look at electronic marketing? Why our Advantage program? Three major reasons.

First, of course, *the benefits to the consumer.* We thought, "What a nice way to provide automatic savings." No need to cut coupons, no need to keep a copy of the ad. Basically, customer convenience. We decided to do whatever we could to enhance customer convenience.

The second major reason was *benefits to Price Chopper.* There's quite an extensive list, but we looked at labor savings. Having shelf talkers on the aisle, near each item, means when a price changed all we had to do was change the tag. We didn't have to change the price on each item, which is a tremendous labor savings to those of us in states that require price marking.

The third major reason was to *enhance our service image.* Development of a database is very important to our business now—getting to know our customers. If they don't have a card, and consumers don't have motivation to use that card, how do you ever get to know your customers and identify them? We've expanded our membership card base to 2.3 million customers for our chain.

We started out with it being a revenue builder for us—from manufacturers. This offered the ability for second brands, if they wanted to put up the money, to get more exposure in our ads and on our shelf talkers. The first phase was to pilot the program, back in 1987-88 when nobody was even talking about this type of concept. Where else to take it but Scranton, Pennsylvania? Nice, isolated area. Demographics weren't too good, given the high age of the population, but we figured we couldn't do much harm out there. The manufacturers that bought into this were primarily the second brands. The primaries didn't need to. So we had a whole lot of advertising with these secondary items.

And what were the results from this first dynamic program? Miserable!! I guess sometimes you have to fail to succeed. We didn't really worry about the appeal of the products from a consumer standpoint. We wanted the revenue from the manufacturers.

Finally, after blaming a lot of other things, we took a look at the items we had. Here were our lead items: light bulbs; ten cents off Hebrew National Deli Mustard; three bean salad; a roller mop. It ended with flashlights. Looking back at it now, obviously it's quite comical. But we're never going to do that again. The cry around the office is "Remember the mustard!"

Early lessons

We started learning that these programs are not going to be revenue makers. We learned that counting on the manufacturers is dangerous. It's time to make this a real part of our marketing program, the temporary price reductions, and make it our primary promotional vehicle, and not to look at the revenue aspects of it—the manufacturer support. Otherwise, you're going to get the wrong manufacturers in there, unless you can move a lot of mustard.....

Getting it right

When we finally started going with the Advantage Program, we tripled our card base, and are still adding thousands of cards a week. We nicknamed it Classic Advantage. It became a real part of our company and our promotional program. We tried again in western Massachusetts and got high ratings from consumers and 93% familiarity with the program. Then, in other areas. Again with high ratings. We saw sales increases, and we saw margins constant or improved. We incorporated the program into our ad: "Take Advantage of Us." We also did radio and television spots.

Consumers gave us high marks, especially on the convenience factor. What they liked best was no coupon clipping. What they liked least was that it was inconvenient—you have to show your card every time, and they didn't like the limit on cover items. As far as the inconvenience goes, if you make it valuable enough, they won't have any problems showing the card. And we expanded the limit on cover items to five.

Customer specific points

To counter the objection to having to use the card each time, what would happen is a manager would override, or the cashiers would use a generic card to give discounts to everyone. *That's what you don't want!* That's what you have to watch out for. Obviously, the answer to it is a customer-specific points program. I mean, you can imagine at an airline ticket counter, if you're on a frequent-flyer program, the person who's selling you the ticket not using your card. You'd be pretty upset if that ever happened. So we got into customer specific points type programs, and did away with that type of problem.

Privacy

Privacy did surface and ended up in the newspaper: "It's not worth giving up my privacy to save a few cents on a roll of paper towels." It really concerned us when we saw that reaction. Again, a small percentage of the database, fortunately. We put together a corporate privacy policy and published it, so there's never any concern that this data will be used by anybody but Price Chopper.

Customer specific marketing

What's in the future? *Customer specific marketing.* Basically, I call it the 11th commandment: "Get to know the customer." Because all consumers are not created equal, it's critical that you do get to know them and merchandise to them in different ways.

Lessons learned

I'll close with lessons learned regarding electronic marketing:

1) Make it your *primary promotional vehicle.* You can't get into this on a half-baked basis. You have to live and breathe it. And not many companies do that.

2) Offer the customer *real value.* Items, prices, services, tie-ins with other merchants. Again, my quote, "Remember the mustard." We'll never make that mitake again.

3) Publish a corporate *privacy policy* so there's never any concern over the use of data.

4) Remember that technology is now driving marketing, not the other way around. Get involved and *understand what these systems can do.*

Customer Loyalty:
Earning it and Rewarding it
Presented by
Feargal Quinn, Managing Director, Superquinn, Dublin, Ireland
at the CIES Young Executives Conference
Bordeaux, France, October 5, 1993

The most important thing that I believe about customer loyalty is that you cannot buy it. Customer loyalty is something that has to be earned.

And there are no short cuts to earning loyalty. Earning loyalty is a long-term task that needs to be at the center of the business all day, every day.

It is only when you have achieved that, only when customer loyalty actually exists, that it makes sense to turn your attention to rewarding loyalty—through the kind of loyalty schemes that we're hearing so much about now.

Rewarding loyalty is the second step; earning loyalty is the first one. And for the second step to make any sense, you have to take the first one beforehand.

But when you have earned loyalty, then you can deepen it, you can reinforce it, you can add to the value of it, by a scheme that is designed to reward the customer for being loyal.

The boomerang principle

My approach to loyalty is based on what I call the "Boomerang Principle," which I explain in my book *Crowning the Customer.* You throw a boomerang, and if you throw it properly, it comes back to you. And in my view, that is what business is all about—getting the customer to come back, again and again.

The Boomerang Principle says that you should run your business with the prime objective of getting your customers to come back again. The prime objective should not be to make the maximum amount of money from them this time, but to make sure that you continue to make money from them in the future.

One of the reasons I developed the Boomerang Principle is I became convinced that you can't afford to buy new customers every week. Every customer you buy through advertising is very, very expensive—you can't possibly cover your costs in doing that from just one visit to your store. To get a proper return from what you invest in attracting new customers, you have got to be able to hold that customer for several visits. So getting them to come in the door is only the first part of the task—the part that advertising can do for you. Getting them to come back through that door next week, and the week after is the part of the task that only you can do— you can do it only through what happens to the customer when she is in the store.

The second main reason I believe in the Boomerang Principle is it focuses attention on your existing customers—who, in my opinion, are the real source of your profit, now and in the future. We tend to get hung up on doing things that will attract new customers, while not paying anything like enough attention to holding on to the ones we have already got. But when you start to run your business on the Boomerang principle, you get your priorities in the right order: you put most of your energy into the customers you already have, most of your energy into persuading them to come back next week...and the week after...and the week after that. In other words, to turn them into "loyal" customers.

Rewarding loyalty

Now if you succeed in earning customer loyalty, then you can start thinking about rewarding it. This is another way to get customers to come back to you. You do it by recognizing and acknowledging their importance to you, by thanking them for being customers, and—most important of all—by giving them a financial incentive to remain as your customer.

Of course, loyalty schemes are as old as the hills. And over the years, they have worked to a greater or lesser extent. But there were always major difficulties. Difficulties that prevented them from coming into the mainstream of retail marketing. Basically, they were clumsy to operate, both from the point of view of the customer and of the retailer. There was always the question: are these things more trouble than they are worth?

What's really exciting now is that the tools and the *know-how* have been developed to create loyalty schemes that are totally customer-friendly. Not alone that, but it's now possible to run loyalty schemes without too much hassle for the retailer, schemes that can be integrated smoothly into the existing operation and which add the bonus of information about customers, which can then be used for targeted marketing. I'm convinced that what we're now looking at is not just another fad, or another tweak, but the beginning of a whole new era in retail marketing.

Technology makes the difference

At the heart of what we are talking about is technology. It is technology that makes it easier for the customer to benefit from the scheme, and easier for the retailer to operate it. But as far as the customer is concerned, all they see of the technology is their loyalty card. This is the key that unlocks the system for them.

Every time they shop with us, they hand their card to the checkout operator. The operator scans the card, and from then on the purchases the customer has made are linked to the customer's identity. It's vital that this business with the card is quick, so it doesn't hold up traffic at the checkouts. It's vital that it's totally dependable—that the card is read successfully the first time, every time. And making sure those things happen is not easy. But once you achieve them, from this simple action of scanning the customer's card, we can tap into a vast amount of new information about the customer.

We already know a lot about the customer—details that she gave us when she registered for the card. Now, each time she shops, we are getting more information—about what she buys, when she buys, how much she spends, and so on. You can see immediately what this opens up—the richness of the marketing possibilities that present themselves, if you know how to harness that information and put it to work.

Rewarding card usage

But of course, that isn't why the customer uses the card. The customer uses the card because we have created a financial incentive for her to do so. By recording her purchases, she is building up credit in our loyalty scheme—credit which can be redeemed later on, in the form of gifts. These gifts are set out in a lavish colour catalogue. They include electrical goods of many kinds, toys, household articles, travel bargains, and so on. The list of rewards was, of course, very carefully researched—and it is refined all the time in the light of actual take-up.

The customer is credited with points according to what she spends, and each gift is exchanged for a number of points that is clearly set out in the catalogue.

Flexibility of points

Now, one of the things I want to draw attention to here is the flexibility that can be built into the system. You can, as we do, give the customers points for every amount they spend. But that is only the starting point. You can then add bonus points on whatever basis you choose. You can offer double points or triple points, or however many points you like, on particular products throughout the store. You can make it possible for customers to build up a very large number of points quickly—but only if they buy particular products.

In this way, you can promote particular lines. Even more to the point, you can get your suppliers to pay for the extra points—because they see it as a powerful way of enhancing the attractiveness of their products in relation to their competition.

We use a two-week cycle for the bonus points promotions—and this means there is a constant change for the customer, which keeps the novelty factor alive and stimulates the interest again and again. But the flexibility you can—and should—build into a system like this goes beyond particular product promotions. You can also incentivize your customers to shop on particular days of the week, or particular times of the day, by offering them extra points to do so. This opens up a whole new vista in terms of controlling the customer flow.

Extending the concept

Now, a further, vastly important part of what we are doing is extending the concept beyond the walls of our own stores. We have recruited other, non-competing retailers who also give points to their customers. So far, these include petrol stations, a chain of cinemas, a chain of furniture and do-it-yourself stores, travel companies—even a bank.

Superquinn is still the hub of the system and is clearly seen as that by all concerned. The points end up on our computer; the customer collects gifts from us. But it is also a powerful promotional tool in its own right for these associated retailers. From our point of view, bringing in the other retailers not only makes it easier for our customers to build up points, but even more important, it also brings us waves of new customers. Because, for instance, if a cinema customer gets a small number of points for buying a cinema ticket, they start to look at the list of other places where they can build up points. Straight away they see how many points they can build up by doing their supermarket shopping with us, and they say, "All right, let's shop at Superquinn next week, since we'll get the points as well."

We have been running this scheme for less than six months, even less as a full-scale scheme. But already it is clear to us that we have a winner. It is attractive to our existing customers and it is bringing us new customers; it is attractive to our suppliers; and it is attractive to the retailers we have gone into partnership with. The result for our bottom line is already positive.

Two requirements for success

In making schemes like this work, two requirements are absolutely key. The first is that *the scheme is genuinely user-friendly*—both customer-friendly and retailer-friendly. That is the real trick here—because if the scheme does not perform in terms of friendliness, it will stop being useful after a short period of time. But properly designed and implemented, these schemes can become a permanent part of a new way of doing things.

The second requirement is also one that I have touched on already: *flexibility*. There is no sense in setting up a system that can only do one thing; can only work in one direction. The system should be designed so that it can take advantage of all the potential that is inherent in this idea. In time, your priorities will change; your customers' interests will change. Your system has to be capable of moving in step, or otherwise it will soon become obsolete.

Customer loyalty is a spectrum

In closing, I want to step back from the technicalities of this system of regarding loyalty and make two fundamental points about the whole issue of bringing customers back to us again and again. The first point is that I think it is useful to look on customer loyalty not as a switch that is on or off, but as a spectrum. The question is not whether customers are loyal or not loyal. The question is *how* loyal they are. If you think of loyalty as a spectrum, stretching all the way from no loyalty at all at one end to absolute total loyalty on the other, then every customer is positioned somewhere along that spectrum.

Our task, day in and day out, is to move every customer further along that spectrum. Whatever their degree of loyalty now, it can be increased. There is no such thing as a customer who is so loyal that we have no further work to do. We have to work to keep them from sliding backwards along the spectrum, and we have to work to keep them moving forward along it.

And the great thing is there is no endpoint to the spectrum, if we are talking about the value of customer loyalty. Even a customer who does all her shopping with us, week after week, can increase in value to us—to the extent that she acts as a missionary for the company among her friends, playing a role in building their loyalty to us or even playing a part in persuading them to come in the door in the first place.

Use technology to help your people

The second general point I want to make has to do with how we look on technology in retailing. There are two, totally opposing ways of seeing technology. The first is to see it as a replacement for people—as a mechanical way of doing what a person had to do before. In the context we're talking about, this approach would see loyalty systems as mechanical ways of stimulating customer loyalty.

The other way of looking at technology, the way I look at it, is as a way of extending the reach of people who serve customers. In other words, you can look on technology as a way of enhancing what people do, a way of increasing the quality of it, a way of broadening the scope of it.

In my view, that is the way to look on these loyalty systems. If we take that view of technology, we will have the right mix, and we will base our approach to building customer loyalty very firmly on the only solid foundation there is: serving the customer's needs.

It's all about serving the customer

Serving the customer is what loyalty is all about. And in the final analysis, only people can give customer service the competitive edge that's the difference between success and failure. In the end, it comes back to people. Helped by technology, certainly. Backed up by technology, extended by technology.

But the crunch factor in customer loyalty is and will always remain people—the people who meet the customers and the people who manage them.

Measured Marketing:
An Update, One Year Later
Presented by
R. Scott Ukrop, Vice President of Marketing,
Ukrop's Super Markets Inc., Richmond, Virginia
at the Food Marketing Institute's Marketechnics
Conference, Houston, February 20, 1995.

Although we've had an electronic marketing program at Ukrop's Supermarket since 1987, we are just at the starting point in *Measured Marketing!* With the *Ukrop's Valued Customer* or *UVC* program, we subscribe to Brian Woolf's recommendations of *rewarding the right customer.* We are looking to reward our customers and enhance our relationship with them by offering them increased savings on the products they buy or are likely to buy.

We've only just begun ...

I say that we are just getting started with *Measured Marketing* because we only began collecting consumer purchase data this past year. Prior to that, we ran an electronic-couponing program that enabled customers to save without clipping coupons. Although such a system was fairly revolutionary in 1987, it is commonplace now. Customers present a card and receive additional savings on specific products. Because the program provides benefits to our customers, our suppliers, and to Ukrop's, it has remained the focal point of our marketing efforts over the years. Our customers save on items throughout our store without having to clip coupons. Our suppliers benefit from a month of display exclusivity in their category and a listing in our monthly newsletter. These activities, combined with the lowest retail price in town (as the savings go directly to the customers), give the manufacturers significant incremental sales.

Ukrop's benefits by reducing the handling cost of thousands of paper coupons resulting from responses to our ads and more important, by maintaining an active mailing list of our customers. This mailing list enables us to communicate with over 290,000 households in the Richmond area!

Cards replace phone numbers

Last year about this time, we began to enhance our UVC program with two major changes. We required customers to present their UVC cards rather than just recite their phone numbers to take advantage of the electronic discounts, and we began tracking their purchases. We had used phone numbers as the basis for customer account numbers since the inception of our program in 1987. This facilitated the process as it allowed customers to receive the electronic discounts even if they didn't have their UVC card with them.

Phone numbers brought with them a series of problems, however. The concern for privacy, for example. Saying the phone number out loud in the checkout line disturbed many customers. Keeping track of changes was another. Customers would move to another address and then give their new phone number, of which we had no record. A number of other customers just gave their phone numbers while never submitting an application form, which still gave them the electronic discounts! And finally, we had mis-keys by cashiers which created unidentified customers in our system. The combination of these problems prompted us, last year, to issue new cards to customers with new permanent numbers, and we requested customers to present their card on each visit.

Sweepstakes

To encourage this change in behavior, we added new benefits or incentives to the program. First, we converted all in-store vendor sweepstakes to be a function of our card. Customers were automatically entered in the sweepstakes whenever they used their UVC card, and they received even more entries by buying the sponsors' products. We gave away cruises, vacations, jeeps, and gift certificates. Our vendors liked this new feature because they could tie in their promotions to actual sales of their products. And our stores liked it because they no longer had to keep up with "entering" pads, boxes, and pens for the sweepstakes. However, we did provide entry forms for customers to mail in their entries, if they didn't want to make a purchase.

5% off certificates

For those customers who said they had never won a contest, we offered yet another incentive. Those households which spent over $1,000 between June 1st and December 31st last year received a certificate good for 5% off any grocery order.

Golden Gift program

As another incentive, we also converted our annual Cash Back to the Community Program, our Ukrop's Golden Gift program, to the card. By using the Valued Customer card, our customers no longer needed to save receipts to give to their favorite non-profit organizations. Their card, in effect, collected the amounts they spent for them. We then issued customers a Golden Certificate in their personally addressed, monthly newsletter. This certificate showed the amount of their total purchases which they, in turn, could give to their participating organization—instead of a pile of register tapes, as in the past.

Targeted offers in monthly newsletter

Our final new benefit was the hardest to communicate, but it was our underlying goal. We wanted to reward our customers through our monthly newsletter with targeted offers. These offers would be for substantial savings on the products they were buying or would be likely to buy. We down-played this concept because of the complexity involved in communicating it to our customers. We intended to rely on word-of-mouth. We wanted our customers to see for themselves that each month, in the newsletter, there was something substantial for them. Once they began to see these useful, relevant offers, they would be sure to use their card every time they shopped and tell their friends and neighbors about the extra benefits.

Communicating the changes

We communicated these changes and new benefits through a series of TV and radio ads, as well as in our stores and newsletters. And to make sure our own associates were on board with the new program, we conducted a series of two-hour meetings for over 1,000 cashiers and courtesy clerks at our Support Center. The advertising and associate training really paid off. The card usage rates did not change substantially, and actually increased over time with 60% of our transactions and 87% of our sales now covered by the card.

Tracking customer behavior

The second major change we made last year was the ability to track our customers' purchase behavior. We installed *MarketExpert*, developed by RMS, a group of former Citicorp people with whom we'd had the privilege of working in our original Valued Customer program. *MarketExpert* allows us to track the data that Brian Woolf detailed in his *Measured Marketing* report. It also allows us to set up behavior groups that represent the areas in which our customers are buying. These behavior groups can consist of total spending, total dollars spent by each household, a store, a department, category, sub-category, all of the manufacturers' products, a group of products defining a lifestyle, such as low-fat items, children's items or infant items or *chocoholics*. Or a single UPC or group of UPC's—however we wish to define them. These groups allow us to track households and target them based on their purchases within these groups.

When the card is used at the checkout, all the purchases fall under these various behavior groups, and we begin to get a picture of the customer's shopping habits. For example, we can see if the customer is a heavy meat purchaser, or if the customer buys sugar-free items, what stores the customer shops in and how often, if the customer responded to a particular offer, and if the customer buys any, say, Coca-Cola products.

Customer specific targeting

Through targeting, we are looking to reward those of our customers who shop with us. We design the offers as a way of saying *thank you* for buying a particular product at Ukrop's. We can vary each newsletter to include the offers *that will be the most meaningful to a particular household*.

Some of these offers might, for example, include a diaper manufacturer giving away baby-wipes after so many diaper purchases, a hot dog manufacturer rewarding his top customers with free dogs for Labor Day, a manufacturer inviting his best customers to a special night at the ball park with the top customer

235

throwing out the first pitch, a Caesar salad mix to top romaine lettuce purchasers, free baby juice to most frequent baby food purchasers, or a free cake to our most frequent greeting card purchasers. Obviously, there are all sorts of ways to reward customers and thank them for their loyalty.

New insights from our database

MarketExpert also allows us to analyze customer transactions in ways that we never previously had at our disposal. We know that 87% of our total sales and 60% of our total transactions are identified or covered with the card. We've learned that we have over 310,000 active households who have shopped with us since June of last year, and over 252,000 customers who have shopped with us in the past twelve weeks.

We know that the top 10% of our customers account for 40% of our total sales and have recently visited our stores 1.8 times per week. We know that 58% of our customers have bought Nabisco products. We've learned that 18.6% have never shopped our HBC department, but on the bright side, only 58 households of our 90,000 top households have never shopped that department. And we know that 1.6% of our total active households have not returned since the first week in June, and 3.6% have not returned since Christmas week.

Better information leads to better decisions

As you can imagine, these numbers begin to give us a clear picture of our business and enable us to manage it more effectively. With this information, we can determine our advertising reach and see what offers brought in new customers to the category. We can also measure which advertising efforts appealed to which segment of our customer base—our *loyals*, our *splits* and our *infrequents*. The sky and, perhaps, our disk space is the limit as to what we can track and study to enhance not only our marketing efforts, but also our merchandising, procurement, and operational efforts.

Our numbers are no different

In the short time that we have been looking at the data, we have had a few surprises. First, our numbers are no different from everyone else's! We had always assumed that because we have some unique offerings and a different marketing strategy, our data would be different from what Brian reported in his study. In fact, the numbers are pretty much the same. A European retailer with whom we shared some numbers reported the same Recency, Frequency and Spending figures for his different customer groups.

We found that 50% of our customers shop, at most, every other week with us and that our attrition rates are close to what Brian reported (and much worse than we suspected!). We can now use this information to try to change the direction of these numbers.

Beware of averages

However, I urge you to beware of averages. In looking at our customer data, we have traditionally looked only at average item values, average order sizes, and straight customer transactions. What do these averages really tell us? As one store manager remarked to me the other day, "If you have one foot in the fire and one foot on a bed of ice, the average is pretty comfortable!" The same is true for what we've learned of customer transactions.

In January, the average customer spent $148 with the UVC card, or $37 per week. However, the top 10% of ourcustomers spent on average $471, with a range of$350 to $3,000 for the month. On the other hand, the bottom 10% spent an average of $8 with a range of $0.50 to $14.50 for the whole month. Clearly, the average hides a lot about the diversity of spending within our individual groups, notwithstanding the diversity of all of our customers. We can now see past the averages and begin to see the impact the different sets of customers have on our business.

Customers like different offers

Customers like to be treated like the individuals that they are. We were pleasantly surprised that our customers did not mind receiving different offers than those of their neighbors. This had been a major concern in our organization. Customers accepted the fact that the offers were based on their purchases. Word-of-mouth has been a great tool in spreading the new benefits of the program. We intend to capitalize on this word-of-mouth as we randomly send out the majority of our various rewards in the form of *surprises* in our newsletters. Although the idea of treating customers differently ran counter to the way we have always done business, when we see that 30% of our customers contribute 76% of our sales, we *know* that all customers are not equal! We can now recognize and reward the customers who are with us day in and day out—those customers whose business is central to our success!

Our 5% certificate to those customers who spent $1,000 is a good example of how we are now differentiating our customer offers. After six months, 80,000 households qualified for the offer. When you consider that 80,000 represents fewer than 28% of our 290,000 active households, perhaps we should be alarmed! However, we know that these 80,000 households contributed to over 73% of our sales during those six months.

Even our best customers love offers

Everyone loves an offer! We were relieved to see that our top customers, who had been receiving the best targeted offers in our newsletters each month, are also the top redeemers of these offers. For a while, I was afraid that the big spenders would not care about coupons, but this has not been the case. Our biggest spenders represent 60% of the users of these offers.

Manufacturer participation

We have found that manufacturers "want in." At first, most manufacturers said to us: "Can you give me the list of all of my competitors' customers?" We told them that wouldn't be any fun! Instead, we showed them the contribution that their top customers make to their sales and we encouraged them to reward those customers. Through substantial offers with which they can control their liability and target directly to their users and potential users, they can thank their *top* customers and make their *split* customers want to be loyal customers of their products.

The targeted offers have proven a great tool for the smaller manufacturers who cannot afford some of our other programs. The coupons lead our customers to the items on the shelf, possibly past displays of their larger competitors. It has been fascinating to see the interest peak within certain categories when one manufacturer finds out we are working with his direct competition.

Surveys vs. behavior

The mouth is mightier than the pen! As much time and effort as we had put into our newsletter to get our message out, it wasn't read as much as we had thought. Surveys showed us that our monthly newsletter readership was extremely hot, but too often, we learned, *people tell you what you want to hear.* The targeted offers have given us a measurement tool to test the readership of the newsletter, and we have seen the readership go up as each month our customers say, "What's in it for me?" However, customers see what they want to, and it has been a real lesson dealing with over 290,000 households one-on-one. Almost as challenging as dealing with the Post Office!

Segmented customer research

Market research shows that you care. By segmenting our customer base, we can target our research and evaluate different products and programs according to users, non-users and the different degrees of usage. For example, we gave our top Kitchen customers a dollar off their next Kitchen purchase and asked for suggestions on items we should make in our Kitchen. Through targeted research, we can get the information we need to serve our specific group of customers better. Not only does this research help us enhance our relationship with our customers, but the very act of speaking to specific customers about the items they buy also shows we care.

The challenge ahead

At Ukrop's, *Measured Marketing* one year later has been a real eye-opener as we begin mining the expansive amounts of data that we have. Our challenge ahead is to make the Ukrop's Valued Customer Program even more worthwhile and to make the best possible use of our information, serving our customers the best we can, so that they will always want to keep coming back.

13

Closing thoughts

As this book has shown, *customer specific marketing* will significantly change the way we go to market and the way we organize our business. We cannot predict the exact path it will take, but the direction is abundantly clear.

In a few years, the practices of today's pioneers will be commonplace. These pioneers are already anticipating this. Some of them are already planning the next phase of this information-based revolution.

There is no one perfect business strategy. The differentiated marketers who win in the long term will be those who internally understand and use their information most effectively and externally keep their programs simple and easy to understand. These retailers will focus all activities around their card (or whatever form of customer identification emerges in the future). They will concentrate on *differentiating* the value that their customers, particularly their best customers, receive, compared to competitive offerings. They will communicate better with their customers and anticipate better their customer needs.

The only limits to where you can take *customer specific marketing* will be in your own creativity—I hope that it will be in a state of constant fermentation!

Index

Books available from Raphel Marketing
12 S. Virginia Avenue, Atlantic City, NJ 08401
Tel: USA (609) 348-6646   Fax: USA +609-347-2455

Customer Specific Marketing...by Brian P. Woolf
A revolutionary new book that describes how retailers are increasing profits by making different offers to different customers. It's the new power in retailing.

Shrinking the Corporate Waistline...by Brian P. Woolf
The book that gives you an inside view of the attitudes and practices of lean retailers. Full of practical money-saving ideas which you will keep referring to.

Crowning the Customer...by Feargal Quinn
The greatest book ever written on customer service by the founder of the world-renowned Superquinn supermarket chain. Learn and apply the secret of the *boomerang principle.*

Up the Loyalty Ladder...by Murray Raphel and Neil Raphel
A special book, full of hundreds of anecdotes and examples, that tells you how you can turn sometime customers into full-time advocates of your business.

Special Fax Order Form

Fax to (USA) (609)347-2455
Raphel Marketing Inc.
12 S. Virginia Ave.
Atlantic City, NJ 08401
Tel: (609) 348-6646

Please send me:
 # copies   **Total**

____ *Customer Specific Marketing* @ $29.95 _____

____ *Shrinking The Corporate Waistline* @ $14.95 _____

____ *Crowning the Customer* @ $19.95 _____

____ *Up the Loyalty Ladder* @ $23.00 _____

____ Plus Postage/Handling $3.50

Total Due $ _____

Please send to:
(Name) _____

(Company) _____

(Street Address) _____

(City) _____ (St.) _____ (Zip) _____

(Country)_____ (Tel): ( ) _____

Credit Card: (check one) ❏ *Visa* ❏ *MC* ❏ *American Express*

Account #: _____ Expires:_____

Cardholder Signature _____

Quantity discounts available. Please call for information.

About the Author

Brian Woolf is a consultant who works with retailers on three continents. Most of his work in recent years has centered on helping retailers gain a competitive edge by taking full advantage of their detailed customer information.

His business life has been centered in retailing in various roles including Deputy Managing Director of Progressive Enterprises, a major New Zealand retailer; Chief Financial Officer of Food Lion, America's low price, low cost supermarket leader; and President of One Price Clothing, a women's discount apparel chain. He is now President of the Retail Strategy Center Inc. based in Greenville, South Carolina.

He is considered one of the leading experts in *customer specific marketing*, speaks extensively on the subject, and is the author of the Coca-Cola Retailing Research Council's 1993 study entitled *Measured Marketing: A Tool to Shape Food Store Strategy*. His earlier book, *Shrinking The Corporate Waistline*, describes the cost-saving practices of leading lean retailers.

He has a Masters degree in Economics and Accounting from the University of Auckland, New Zealand, and an MBA from the Harvard Business School.

If you are interested in more information on the concepts in this book, please contact:

Retail Strategy Center, Inc.
6 Parkins Lake Court,
Greenville, South Carolina 29607-3628, USA
Tel: (864) 458-8277   Fax: +864-458-8144